Praise for

'This book is

party that you won't be leaving soon. I believe we're living in a time of fresh erasures, systemic violences working that global pandemic to take some other bodies out. Looking so freshly at the history of queerness, sexual deviance and the long long coordinated erasures of colonialism, bigotry and transphobia the essential non binary nature of art opens up right here like the wildly singing flower it is and So Mayer's compelling version makes sense, makes me listen.' Eileen Myles

'In a time of rising fascism, So Mayer highlights ways that artists have found strategies of resistance, and offers hope in historical analysis.' Juliet Jacques

'A book of thoughts for an emergency – that is to say, for today – that is absolutely worth reading with haste, but not in a hurry.' B Ruby Rich

A catalogue record for this book is available from the British Library.

First published in 2020 by Peninsula Press

400 Kingsland Road

E8 4AA

London

peninsulapress.co.uk

Printed in Great Britain by CPI Group (UK) Ltd, Croydon

2 4 6 8 10 9 7 5 3 1

ISBN-13: 9781913512026

A Nazi Word for a Nazi Thing

So Mayer

PENINSULA PRESS, LONDON
POCKET ESSAYS

It is a photograph he never took, no one here took it.

...

[Geryon] flicks Record.
This is for Ancash, he calls to the earth
diminishing below. This is a memory of our
beauty. He peers down
at the earth heart of Icchantikas dumping all
its photons out her ancient eye and he
smiles for
the camera: 'The Only Secret People Keep.'
— Anne Carson, *Autobiography of Red*

It is a photograph of something he never saw: his life's work, on fire.

It is not a photograph, but a still from a black-and-white Pathé newsreel. A uniformed soldier with his back to the camera throws books so hard that they appear to hang like ravens above a vast bonfire, around which more books and papers are scattered on the street.

History tells us of the Jewish books destroyed in Berlin's Opernplatz on 10 May 1933. Soldiers and Hitler Youth burned 25,000 books before a crowd of over 40,000 people, part of an attempt to eradicate all thought and writing condemned as *entartet*: degenerate and un-German. Among those books were thousands taken, four days earlier, from the library, research and community centre run by Magnus Hirschfeld, a German Jew. But these books were not burned only because they were Jewish.

Hirschfeld's Institut für Sexualwissenschaft ran from 1919 until the looting and burning of

1933. It was the first-ever research institute to focus solely on human sexuality. The books taken so violently from its Berlin site, which comprised a library, cinema and cabaret, included the first academic studies written by and about lesbian, gay, bisexual, intersex and trans people, as well as diaries and personal testimonies, novels, poetry, visual arts, and popular magazines: a whole culture of self-defining queerness – complete with internecine wrangles and scandals – that had Berlin as its epicentre.

Because we only have the ashes, the history of that thriving culture is only just being reconstructed today.

Because Hirschfeld's work was done defiantly in public, and sought to challenge and change dominant cultural values, the Nazis branded it *entartet*. Derived from Linnaean and Darwinian biology, the term is typically translated into English as *degenerate*, a word that also has its roots in biology, and particularly in eugenics. It means, strictly, that which does not have a classification (*artet*), that which is excluded from the set of all sets – not just degenerate but de-genred, impossible to classify and therefore impossible to (be permitted to) exist. The term eradicates what it (un)names: a form of absolute censorship that erases even the *imaginative possibility* of an individual, community or idea. In Hirschfeld's expansive vision of human genders and sexualities – in the abundance of publications and performances and persuasions that he fostered – the Nazi regime found the exact opposite of its own totalitarianism. Hence its totalising obliteration.

Hirschfeld learned about the destruction of the Institut and its library from the newsreel. He saw it by chance before the main feature in a cinema in Paris, where he was doubly in exile from the Nazi regime, as a Jew and as a gay man. Even in exile, he kept writing and publishing, including a tract against racism. He never returned to Berlin. And his work faced a similar exile.

His reflexively titillating guide *Berlin's Third Sex* (1904) only made it into English translation in 2017, and his monumental *The Sexual History of the World War* (1930) languished out of print for sixty years, from its first English-language publication in 1946 until 2006. Its title expresses Hirschfeld's belief that sexology was not just a prurient fascination with that which was deemed aberrance, but a methodology that could bring new understanding to complex social and historical phenomena by attending to the granular detail of embodied and affective experiences. Section titles such as 'Amatory Adventures of Female Spies', 'Eroticism Behind Military Drill', 'Propaganda and Sex Lies' and 'The Bestialization of Man' affirm that Hirschfeld was not above arousing his readers' curiosity, while the final chapter, 'Post-War Revolution and Sexuality', underlines the radically transformative aim behind his stimulating prose. Championing feminism, class struggle, and the end of empire, he noted that the war had re-routed rather than dispelled them. 'No matter how catastrophic the changes of the World War were', he wrote hopefully, 'we must regard these alterations as a continuation of previous developments' in the movement towards revolution.

For Hirschfeld, the confluence of gender and sexuality was *the* place where the individual and social intersected, because of desire. It was desire that moved gender identity and sexuality from just being a set of subjective experiences to an interconnecting web of social trajectories, and thus a potentially revolutionary force. He collected thousands of personal testimonies – precursors to his patient Lili Elbe's well-known *Man Into Woman* (published posthumously in 1933) – to inform his forging of a collective European LGBTIQ+ history. His first (pseudonymous) publication, driven by the suicide of a patient, was called *Sappho and Socrates* (1896), a startling call to arms that followed the work of decadent poets such as Algernon Swinburne in seeking out the traces of a queer and sex-positive history in European culture.

Hirschfeld's work at the Institut began in the decadent milieu of fin-de-siècle Berlin. As described by Robert Beachy in *Gay Berlin*, it was a city of dense backstreets and open parklands, a city full of bars and clubs where underpaid soldiers did survival sex work in defiance of sodomy laws, while the police chief was either unusually tolerant or looking to protect certain royal family members and aristocrats from the blackmail that was epidemic. After the Great War, as the city sought its former glories and gloryholes, tourist marks – and their hyperinflating Marks – generated not just survival but revival for a queer subculture suddenly in the spotlight. Both pleasure and economic necessity had long been the othermothers of queer Berlin's underground inventions.

It was in this transitional, chaotic moment that Hirschfeld turned to cinema, itself a transitional, chaotic technology that had arrived in 1895. By 1919, cinema still stood for modernity; yet to settle into Hollywood contours, it still fizzed with avant-garde possibility. Hirschfeld co-wrote and appeared as himself in the earliest-known feature film to openly depict gay male sexuality, *Different from the Others*

(*Anders als die Andern*, Richard Oswald, 1919), made in the revolutionary aftermath of the war. The film got caught up in arguments about Paragraph 175, the anti-sodomy statute against which Hirschfeld had written his first pamphlet, and after a successful public run it was confined to private screenings. Focusing on the devastating effect of blackmail under Paragraph 175, the film contains the earliest film footage of a drag club and of same-sex dance partners, as well as an appearance by Hirschfeld as the Doctor, giving a series of lectures, via intertitles, arguing that the full spectrum of gender and sexuality is natural. 'Those that say otherwise', the Doctor argues, 'come only from ignorance and bigotry.'

It was this ignorance and bigotry that pushed the film back into the closet after its successful public outing. Most of the forty prints were stored at the Institut because they could only be used for private screenings, and this led to their destruction: they were among the reels that burned in Opernplatz.

However, Hirschfeld's pedagogical bent meant that forty minutes of the film survived, since he had edited its lecture scenes into a subsequent film project. A scientific documentary about other-than-human sexuality, *Laws of Love* (*Gesetze der Liebe*, 1927) was able to circumvent censorship, circulating within a small, educational circuit that included Hirschfeld's own lecture tours. In the 1920s, a print of the documentary somehow found its way to the Soviet Union and was subsequently spotted in the archives after its collapse. Between 2011 and 2013 – nearly a century after *Different from the Others*' original release – UCLA film archivist Jan-Christopher Horak oversaw a project that used the rediscovered documentary in order to reconstruct a partial version of *Different From the Others*.

Before that, the film owed its cultural status to its having been reviewed and remembered. It is thus often cited as an indirect influence on blackmail drama *Victim* (Basil Dearden, 1961), the first British fiction feature to use the word 'homosexual'; following the 1957 Wolfenden Report, Dearden set out to change attitudes toward homosexuality, and the film is credited with influencing the partial decriminalisation in 1967. How and when Dearden or producer Michael Relph might have seen or heard of *Different from the Others* is the subject of speculation. Having never been screened outside Germany and the Netherlands, its potential influence was limited in its time, and halted utterly after its destruction in 1933. An imaginative space was foreclosed that is only now being reopened, with the insurgence of an assertive activist transnational LGBTIQ+ community that is able to turn to archives made available by digitisation. As Sandy Stone has frequently argued – and as Hirschfeld would certainly have agreed – trans and queer people have been at the forefront of activist technological developments, seeking not only our own formations in the present but also to extend them reparatively across histories.

Hirschfeld's lifework was attentive to the potential of mass communications technologies

– magazines and paperbacks, radio and cinema – to create wide-reaching and wide-ranging conversations about gender and sexuality. Like many utopian thinkers and filmmakers of his time, Hirschfeld believed that cinema would revolutionise how people related to one another, once they had seen themselves with new eyes. Cinema, too, was different from other cultural forms: in the silent era, it spoke an international, embodied language that was thought to need no translation. Unlike theatre and opera, it did not require costly live performances. It could reach huge audiences who would be transformed.

He was right. But it was not the radical Expressionist artists of Weimar cinema who, always making space for ambiguities and pluralities, would be the ones to realise cinema's totalising potential to its fullest: it would be the Nazis, the party and politics that burned Hirschfeld's books and drove him into exile. Most famously through the work of Leni Riefenstahl, the Nazis recognised and exploited cinema's power to enrapture in order to propagandise against those who were 'different from the others', and eventually to secure – and record – their erasure.

After all, Hirschfeld watched his film burn on film.

△

Hirschfeld was not alone in encountering – being at once implicated in and alienated from – his own history as a Pathé projection. News reels us, and reels us in. Whether we realise it or not, in the Anglophone world, when we think of Nazi Germany and the Second World War, we often see it within the frame of a British Pathé newsreel, a form that defined and continues to define how we see the first half of the twentieth century. Although the events that they record are now history, the reels continue to define 'the news'.

Newsreels screened before features in the Western world for several decades, creating an implicit hierarchy: fact before fiction, the real before the imagined, linear time over flashbacks and dreams. At the same time, they offered a conformist script for reading the film to come, a reality test for the mores and temporalities of the action.

To paraphrase Chimamanda Ngozi Adichie, having a single frame through which to see history is dangerous. Not least because Pathé embedded itself as an objective record: as *the* archive. As the Allies' archive, Pathé also came to be seen as in itself anti-fascist, not least in its claims to objectivity, even as it also presented propagandistic, militaristic, morale-boosting reports. Yet the Pathé newsreel did not explain, for its audience, which books were being burned and what they contained.

My education within the British school system replicated the Pathé newsreel version of history. The lessons may have been called History, English, Science but they were all the same blasé inculcation of imperialism and militarism as part of a national identity. They were an eradication, redoubled by the wilful Thatcherite eradication of society, of complexity, of connection and of the possibilities that lay in being 'different from the others'.

This is a history I never learned, because no one taught me: my history.

Fascism depends on the inscription of a single story told in linear time. Burned books stay burned. Burned peoples remain ash. Coming up against the newsreel image of these books being burned confronts me not only with grief in relation to the histories I had been taught, but also those I had been deprived of. I remember an assembly from my final year at school, held on the first Holocaust Remembrance Day, 27 January 1996, fifty-one years after the liberation of Auschwitz. The headteacher read by rote an official list of the communities who had been imprisoned and murdered in the camp – which she pronounced Aus-wich – omitting only LGBTIQ+ people. I remember vividly the feeling of silent fury as I waited through the repeated mispronunciation, through the list. A fury silenced by her silence.

I don't know how or where I first encountered the LGBTIQ+ histories of the Nazi era.

Learning furtively, in fragments, means I cannot reconstruct an intellectual genealogy prior to this incendiary instance of rage. The fury does not trail a remembered reading list in its wake; that is part of its grief. I couldn't speak because I had no one to speak with. There is no newsreel that unreels, just this one frame. When I was first encountering my own difference, I had no Dr Hirschfeld to listen to me and teach me through intertitles, as Paul Körner (Conrad Veidt) does in *Different From the Others*. I had no idea how to, or whether I could, pull histories and possibilities I didn't then know existed out of the fire, or even catch their ashes.

This is my heritage as a European queer and genderqueer non-binary person, just as much as the Sho'ah is for me as an Ashkenazi Jew. My 1980s education at a British Jewish primary school and at Hebrew school in a profound and problematic sense revolved around the Sho'ah, and its legacy, as intrinsically and essentially Jewish phenomena; as phenomena intrinsic and essential to my identity as a Jew, and to centring European Jewishness within my identity. To make any other claim, to live an identity that defied the strictures of conservative Judaism which, like many other orthodox institutional faiths, is homophobic and transphobic, would be 'to do the Nazis' work for them', in the words I was taught at home, at synagogue and at school.

I had been cut off from histories that might have helped me feel a sense of community and continuity within the deeply homophobic (as well as insidiously anti-Semitic) Thatcherite Britain of my childhood. As an adult able to learn these histories through an emergent wave of exhibitions, films, novels, scholarly works and activism, I was confronted with the larger question of what happens when histories are foreshortened, homogenised and smoothed over; and with my responsibility for their recovery in all their complexity.

Confronting the newsreel image of these books being burned, I felt that those books had been burned again, or their ashes trampled upon, by those who educated me. Their history – their identity – had been elided. To refuse to name the lesbian, gay, bisexual, intersex and trans people who were sent to concentration camps, subsequently sent to prison, or went into hiding for decades after the war is to do the Nazis' work for them.

Retelling the stories of Hirschfeld's encounter with his own self-destruction on screen, and my encounter with it, does not require straight biography, nor is it consigned to fragmentation. To redress the Nazis' work of erasure, I want to take up Julian Carter's phrase 'folds of time', which they use to encompass the process and effects of gender transition, in which personal memory folds back on itself, as fuller versions of one's own history are shared.

What is fragmented by fascism is folded by gender/queerness. Fascism insists on and through its authoritarian history, eradicating any contesting accounts, especially personal and cultural memories. A non-linear experience of gender or sexuality, which 'folds' me back into re-evaluating childhood experiences of my self and its context, teaches me how to gather and be gathered by a complex history. Weimar Berlin rises up when it is invoked and entwined in the AIDS activism of the 1980s and 1990s, via the recovery work of the gay liberation movement of the 1970s. It is through this recovery work that I have been able to access Hirschfeld's history.

In a movement and community where still too few activists and artists survive to be elders, the real queer and trans coming of age is not coming out, but coming to recovery work: first as a viewer or reader finding themselves, then as a participant in the archives. We enfold queer texts and traces into our memories so we can pass them on.

In this folding, I want to take up lesbian writers Nicola Griffith's and Kelley Eskridge's term QUILTBAG (queer, intersex, lesbian, trans, bisexual, asexual and gay) to use from hereon out. This acronym disrupts the expected order of dissident sexual and gender identities, for which the common Anglophone acronym has come to seem like a hierarchy rather than an umbrella. QUILTBAG recalls the AIDS Memorial Quilt, one of the best-known acts of queer resistance, one that was crafty, angry, social and widespread. And I also use QUILTBAG in homage to Ursula K. Le Guin's essay on 'the carrier bag theory of fiction', another narrative disruption wherein she calls attention to the non-linear and associative, to the connective, capacious and chaotic – to the kinds of echoes and recursions, folds and detours that describe feminist and queer histories as they are interrupted by persecution and forced into repetition, but also as they are connected across time and space by the work of looking different(ly).

QUILTBAG offers the gentleness, the needful

holding that the queer community extends to these non-linear histories that mix and jumble and sit close to one another even if they may not quite touch. This essay is about hard, sad, sharp, painful histories of oppression and the incredible tough tenderness of queer resistance in its ability to contain and to collate. It's an attempt at a QUILTBAG, a patchwork that is raw around the edges with trying to think some of these histories together; a patchwork that I hope you will add to.

Silence is self-replicating. Postwar governments and cultures, which enforced social conservatism as necessary and unchallengeable in the service of reconstruction, silenced QUILTBAG survivors of the Nazi regime. When the Nazis burned the Institut's books, they burned both the histories they reported and the history of their creation, the work of quilting the bag that could hold the community that it named, a community whose continuity from ancient cultures into our future the Institut was enabling, documenting and protecting. The burning was almost entirely effective. Until the last few decades, Weimar's resistant queer culture and its suppression have both been – outside of QUILTBAG culture itself – largely hidden from view.

When we exclude QUILTBAG narratives and communities from radical and antifa history, we do the Nazis' work for them. Equally, when we characterise persecution as an act consigned to a Nazi past. Their persecution of QUILTBAG people, like their persecution of Jews, Roma, Black people (particularly and emblematically jazz musicians), communists, anarchists, disabled people and sex workers, was an extreme form of the same prejudices that were already – and remain – social norms. In Nazi terminology, all these people were grouped together – or rather, erased together – under the heading of a single term: *entartet*.

By grouping so many different kinds of people under the term degenerate, and associating that term with un-Germanness, the Nazis enforced an ideology of total erasure. *Entartet* at once named and denied difference; it refused nuance while claiming to have its basis in the objective reading of nuances of physical appearance and biological heritage. Functionally an adjective, it comes to be used in place of the noun *Entartung*, degeneration or degeneracy. Nazism is a grammar of turning descriptors into designations, fixed identities marked permanently on the body. *Entartet* encapsulates the fascist reduction of the complexity of identification, heritage and lived experience to a stamp: not only because it was used to fix rather than describe, but because it means something indescribable. It was an identity without identity, a denial of the right to self-identity and an assertion of the state's power to identify. *Entartet* stops the mouth, takes away the words you have for yourself, and then uses them to destroy you.

Δ

It is (a photograph by) a person, or people, who never existed, no one here knows they exist.

The Nazi investment in the biological was so great they even saw it expressed in aesthetic practices. In order to imprint un-Germanness on a mass audience, in 1937 they mounted a blockbuster exhibition: *Entartete Kunst*, Degenerate Art.

Actually, they called it *Entartete 'Kunst'*. Viewers entered with the works' right to be called art already in question. One of Joseph Goebbels' pet projects, it was staged, stagily, in the Munich Institute of Archaeology, which held numerous plundered works, including many sculptures from areas of Africa colonised by Germany before and during WWI. These sculptures were similar to those in the Louvre whose forms Pablo Picasso had expropriated; the *entartet* designation enthusiastically embraced modernism's already problematic fetishisation of non-European art, in order to confuse and condemn.

Viewers knew what to expect in a museum, especially a museum of archaeology: dead things, distant cultures, decontextualised so they could be consumed. *Entartete 'Kunst'* granted this, pinning and vitrifying the multifarious world of modernist art. Here were the most challenging, alive works of the era – pickled in a jar. However, the taxonomical project of the museum, of archaeology – of European science – was shown up by the staging. Rather than presenting modernism within the cool, objective framing of the museum, the layout of the exhibition reproduced the fanatical illogic underlying fascism, as it deployed a system of non-categories in a rigidly categorical manner.

The first three rooms were themed by non-themes, a series of escalating and mutually reinforcing propagandistic frames designed to influence how visitors saw the works. In the first room were works considered to demean Christianity, such as Ludwig Gies' (now lost) Expressionist crucifix – as a dog whistle reminder that (in Christian tradition) the Jews crucified Christ. In 1937, Nazism presented itself as secular and even anti-clerical, but it could not pass up on an opportunity to exploit both Catholic anti-Semitism and nationalism. This moral framework would impress itself on visitors through the repeated, subliminal connection between Jewishness and modernist art's degeneracy. It turned the exhibition into a kind of auto-da-fé through which they could purge – and prove they had purged – themselves not only of any traces of sympathy with Jews, but also of any interest in modernist art.

The works by Jewish artists in the second room would then be read, in sequence, as implicitly demeaning Christianity. The third room's works were described as insulting to German people, specifically women, soldiers and farmers, who were collectively the embodiments and practitioners of *blut und boden*, the central Nazi platform of 'blood and soil', formulated in contrast to the stereotype of Jewish 'rootless cosmopolitanism'. Thus works that insulted *blut und boden* were implicitly by Jewish or Jewish-aligned artists, which thereby re-inscribed the Jewish artists in the previous room as necessarily anti-German. The very idea of *entartet* as a designation for un-Germanness was predicated on anti-Semitism, and anti-Semitism was a manifestation of the world-destroying force of imperialist racism.

Subsequent rooms underlined the sense of escalation by having no themes and no logic.

The haphazard hanging dramatised a significant element of how *entartet* was being shifted from a descriptor to a fixed denominative: that degeneracy was infectious. Paintings were hung three or four deep, with no regard for the size of the work, and often crookedly, above and over door frames. In some galleries they were surrounded by simplistic and nonsensical slogans painted on the walls that appropriated, and mocked, both Dadaist presentation and the startling intertitles of Expressionist and Soviet cinema. Those forms' radical intentions are turned back in on themselves, part of an intentionally pornographised spectacle of undifferentiated mingled bodies and voices mounted one upon the other.

The exhibition used pornographic aesthetics to imply that the artists were all sexual deviants. It made specific reference to the homosexuality of some of the artists exhibited, without distinguishing presumed and proven, and interpreted some of the works as homosexual in content, often deliberately confusing Hirschfeldian terminologies for sexuality and freely applying the capacious non-categorisation of *entartet*.

Entartet works by decontextualisation. It is an erasure of what makes the works work; what makes them art. Without their community context, the invective caricatures of Weimar artists such as George Grosz were presented as documentary – or even as advertisement – rather than as the critique they were. Where Weimar artists used the erotic to criticise the corruption of capitalism, Nazi ideology reframed corruption as innate to marginalised communities. Abstraction was not presented as an aesthetic and critical choice, but rather cited as evidence that the artists must have inherent and inherited degeneracies, both physical and intellectual, that prevented normative perception. Stripping modernists' formal strategies of their political charge of punching-up and speaking truth to power, the Nazi propaganda machine gleefully presented these works as yet more evidence of deviancy and degeneration.

This mocking recontextualisation was successful far beyond any previous presentation of modernism, travelling to twelve German cities. Archive photographs of more than 20,000 works confiscated by Goebbels (of which only 600–800 were exhibited) show a marked emphasis on nudes. This was not mere salaciousness or salesmanship. It was a deliberate strategy. The emphatic and alienating foregrounding of the body – of the body as a sexual body and of the sexual body as a diseased mind-body – forcibly emphasised embodiment to the point of incoherence. The body as abstraction activates and permits the erasure of living bodies. Display objectifies, becoming erasure.

It is a photograph of works that no one was meant to see, nor to see who took them.

Some viewers might have claimed they were only there to see the great works of European modernism that had been withheld from them by private (read: Jewish) collectors. It was one of the first opportunities in Germany to see the work of German and international art superstars displayed together: home-grown (un-)German artists like Otto Dix, Grosz, Kirchner, Paul Klee, Max Liebermann, Franz Marc, Emil Nolde and Kurt Schwitters cheek-by-jowl with Marc Chagall, Wassily Kandinsky, Piet Mondrian and Picasso. These were the very artists who had redefined the field, a fact that the exhibition denied by placing 'art' in quotation marks, creating an optical illusion, a kind of doubled vision that blended tourism and voyeurism.

The quotation marks in the title, like the chaotic hanging, disinfected the work, creating a sanitised setting in which viewers could experience the thrill of the illicit while also disavowing it. Passing through the exhibition thus became – was sold as – an inoculation: a small, necessary dose of what was designated *entartet* that would guarantee the visitor's long-term health. This allowed viewers to both see and not see the actual works of art, their labour to reframe the world; it allowed them to 'collect' an experience they told themselves they had been denied, and to deny it, in its fullness, to themselves.

The exhibition was curated to encourage the infuriated sense of exclusion and entitlement on which Nazism capitalised. Sometimes the text panels in the exhibition included the artist's race. Sometimes the effect was achieved by less direct means. The panels always noted how much the painting or sculpture had sold for, with the figures not adjusted downwards to compensate for the hyper-inflation of the late 1920s. As all money was understood within Nazi ideology as being Jewish money, the implication was that even where a work's artist was not Jewish, the art market that had inflated its value was. Thus all modernism could be considered to be Jewish modernism – a scam that tricked, stole from and humiliated the German people, even when no Jewish artists or curators were involved in a work's production or exhibition. It was an optical illusion: not art, but stolen money stuck to the walls.

It is not a painting and no one made it: that is the operational power of *Entartete 'Kunst'*. Most cruelly, it used the radical representational strategies used by artists themselves to question industrial capitalism and imperialism – strategies that might be grouped as *Verfremdungseffekt*, or alienation effect – to strip them of their own identity, creativity and right to self-determination. Similarly, fixing *entartet* as a designation used the very disciplines that Hirschfeld and others had been trying to renew

Ein sehr aufschlußreicher
rassischer
Querschnitt

Man beachte besonders auch die unten stehenden drei Malerbildnisse. Es sind von links nach rechts: Der Maler Morgner, gesehen von sich selbst. Der Maler Radziwill, gesehen von Otto Dix. Der Maler Schlemmer, gesehen von E. L. Kirchner.

in order to close down their more inclusive vision of humanity. *Entartet*, as a label, homogenised biology, psychology and sociology into a simplistic proposition: that those of us being demonised and excluded are our bodies, and – because those bodies are nothing – nothing more.

There is a reversal of categories. On the one hand, qualities that had been argued by Hirschfeld as facts of biology are presented as cultural, as in the Nazis' pre-1929 propaganda that claims that queerness and transness are a 'Jewish plot'; on the other, cultural phenomena such as political allegiance and aesthetic practices are defined as biological 'facts' – deviant and pathological – in line with eugenic ideology.

Entartet is bad biology, but not in the sense that the Nazis meant, just as it is bad grammar, but not in the way they meant. In the all-consuming usage of *entartet*, *artet* (classification) disappears: the idea of the 'degenerate' erases the very idea of genre. *Entartet* could be defined by the confusion it purposefully generates, as that which makes classification impossible. *Entartet* – the term itself, and the term's shift from adjectival to nominative as metonymic for the Nazis' dual practices of eugenics and linguistic erasure – was able to mobilise biologism because biology as a Western science was already mired in racism, sexism, ableism, classism, homophobia and transphobia; it proceeded not from 'objectivity' but from, and in order to uphold, the prejudices of the time in which it was developed. Charles Darwin did not know how to analyse the evidence, described in his notebooks, of a wide range of genders and sexualities in the animal kingdom often linked to co-operative rather than competitive behaviours. So he stripped it of context and specificity, and misrepresented it in accordance with both Christian morality and colonial philosophy as nature 'red in tooth and claw'. The Nazis are not misapplying Darwinian ideas; they are following through on their exclusionary logic.

Entartet is a Nazi word for a Nazi thing: an idea of difference that strategically presents itself as biological in order to both authenticate and obfuscate deep-rooted prejudice, to confuse the conversation and silence criticism. Its sleight of mind erases argument: defending itself as science on the one hand, while deriding incompatible scientific findings as cultural warfare. Now you see it; now you can't.

It is an image that no one saw: no one woman.

Entartet did not arise in a vacuum. It is a way of seeing; a persistence of vision.

While many of the optical illusions known as ambiguous figures are composed of alternating black-and-white geometric shapes, one of the best-known examples depends on perceptions of normative femininity. Known as 'my wife or my mother-in-law', the image has been dated back to an 1888 German postcard, although the title came from American cartoonist William Ely Hill's 1915 version. Studies show that viewers' perception is affected by their peer group: by the faces that surround them, and that they acknowledge as valued or valid. Despite a century of studies demonstrating that perception is not only subjective, but structurally and systemically limited, it is still reported as news that facial recognition algorithms, which are programmed predominantly by middle-class white cis men feeding computers data they consider both objective and normative, are dangerously biased. There is no ambiguity in the ambiguous image; there are only the non-choices presented by white supremacy and heteropatriarchy.

The figure moved from popular humour to experimental psychology via American psychologist Edwin Boring's paper 'An Ambiguous Figure'. Like many of the disciplines that emerged in the late nineteenth century, psychology was informed by the need to standardise both how people saw and how they were seen: to create hierarchies predicated on fixed classifications of the normal and the pathological. *Entartet* did not arise in a vacuum, but in an international scholarly conversation among imperial nations wherein a scientific method developed that was predicated on inherent bias, solely to establish white supremacy. It was English scientist Francis Galton who coined the term eugenics in 1883, based on the concept of 'survival of the fittest' made famous by Darwin, his cousin. Building on Thomas Hobbes' philosophy of the 'war of all against all', Galton outlined a supremacist breeding programme for creating what Friedrich Nietzsche would call the *Übermensch*, the superman.

Galton argued that eugenicist practices were necessary not just to tilt evolution in favour of European nations, but because they were at risk from what was called degeneracy, which was often traced to the influence of the nations that Europeans were colonising. Racism, Orientalism and anti-Semitism, particularly as expressed through the fear of interracial sexual alliances, were legitimated by claims that the 'white race' – a construct produced by eugenics – would first degenerate, and then (again using a Darwinian concept) become 'extinct'. *Entartet* has always been an ambiguous figure, apparently capacious and all-consuming, yet always putting the same face on white heteropatriarchy's anxieties.

No sooner had homosexuality and gender dissidence been named and formulated by European thinkers such as Oscar Wilde, than they were subsumed into degeneracy, and connected insidiously and repeatedly to 'the Orient'. Jewish men were inscribed as effeminate in Victorian popular culture; Jewish women as simultaneously excessively feminine, and as masculinised, because they were perceived as hypersexual. As Sander Gilman has explored, Jewishness was insistently inscribed as visible and embodied, with caricatures extending far beyond noses into gendered and sexual expression. In other words, if they wanted to assimilate, Jews had to 'prove' they weren't genderqueer.

In George Eliot's novel *Daniel Deronda*, written two years before Galton's *Hereditary Genius* in 1876, the eponymous Jewish hero rejects his mother when he eventually finds her. She is the stereotype of Oriental(ised) Judaism, a hypersexual, dark-haired, dark-skinned Sephardi woman who has been – has allowed herself to be – exploited. Deronda's rejection seeks to replace his 'dark' Jewish origin with proto-Zionism, presented in nationalist, heteronormative terms. He saves, secularises and then marries a young Orthodox Jewish woman in order to father a newly muscular, militant, Westernised Judaism. Eliot, intentionally or not, shows how *entartet* could be internalised by its excluded subjects in their search not only to secure posterity but also to reconfigure what was considered hereditary.

So it is perhaps unsurprising that it was a Jewish art historian, Max Nordau, who, a few decades before the Nazis' ascendance and on the rising tide of imperialism, first brought the word *entartet* across from biology into cultural studies. In the two volumes of *Entartung* (*Degeneration*, 1892–93), Nordau – birth name Simon Südfeld, son of a rabbi – turned to eugenicist language in his attempt, like Deronda, to reject 'Old-World' Judaisms and to assimilate into middle-class high culture. Nordau's book appeared in English translation just months before Wilde's sentencing in 1895, running to seven editions in six months. His condemnation of Wilde as a degenerate symptom of the decline of English masculinity (for which he cited as evidence British losses during the Boer

War), was widely quoted as justification for the outcome of the trial.

A social conservative, Nordau used *entartung* to harangue the decadence he perceived in late nineteenth-century art movements such as Symbolism. Like many humanities scholars, he attempted to legitimate his views through the application of pseudo-scientific language and criteria. On the basis of Nietzsche's biography, he made the spurious claim that 'degenerate' art practices emerged from disabilities or illnesses assumed to be hereditary, and whose nineteenth-century aetiologies blurred the physical and the intellectual.

The Nazis took up the philosophy of a secular Jewish art historian who deliberately used *entartung* to argue *against* anti-Semitism (specifically, in the case of Richard Wagner, that it was symptomatic of degenerate hysteria), and repurposed it to argue that it wasn't degeneracy but *Jewishness* that was the problem in modern culture. The Nazis used Nordau's theory to rehabilitate the non-Jews Nietzsche and Wagner, and to undergird the persecution of artists on the basis of their actual or perceived ideological Jewishness. The tortuous, circular illogic shows up the nakedly expeditious nature of the Nazi regime in all its cynical manipulations of ideology.

It's another kind of ambiguous figure, where Nazi ideology claims it can see the biological in the psychological, and vice versa. Racialisation, sexuality, gender identity, disability, neurodivergence, poverty and criminal convictions all become connected to, and interpreted through, fixed visual traits whose meaning is recursively identified through their association with these *entartet* categories. Can you see it? If you can't, it's because you inhabit one of those categories. There's no biology here, just a double bind in which dominant culture sees what it wants to see, then marshals 'evidence' to silence any potential critics by subsuming them.

The emergence of late nineteenth-century European culture is inextricably entwined with the imperialism that funded and framed it. This makes any naïve recourse to sexology for liberation vexed, just like any embrace of European modernism. Sexology, including that of Hirschfeld, originates in colonial racism; the modern concept of the sex/gender binary arises from studies intended to prove the claim that race is biological. Cinema, too, is a double bind: Hirschfeld turned to the moving image as a technology offering radical possibilities for seeing anew in order to support queer liberation. Yet he was also entering into a fraught relationship with a tool that, like sexology, emerged from and perpetuated white supremacy, and whose supremacist practices would record the destruction of his work.

Motion pictures are an optical illusion. Analogue cinema depends on persistence of vision, a neurological trick that turns twenty-four still frames per second into a moving image. Relying on a socio-political version of the trick, cinema has inscribed itself as always having been there, the key witness at every moment of human history, through its combination of fictional stagings and documentary observation. The Société Pathé Frères emerged from the locus classicus of cinema, fin-de-siècle Paris, where the Frères Lumières had laid the groundwork for a medium that, in order to sell, would merge the documentary and the fantastical, reframing quotidian events like the arrival of a train as thrilling spectacles. It's this conjuncture – this market-driven imperative – that allows Pathé to describe WWII as its 'golden age', profiteering by converting real-life battle scenes into 'some of the most dramatic material ever captured on film by a newsreel company'.

Cinema is, in fact, war by other means. There are few industrial materials, outside of weapons manufacture, as unstable and dangerous as nitrate film, nitrocellulose, on which silent cinema and much early sound cinema was shot until the 1950s. It began life as a weapon, an explosive and propellant known as guncotton, first used by the Confederates in the American Civil War; at the same time and on the same battlefields, the same compound – known as collodion – was being used to take some of the first war photographs, using the rearranged bodies of dead soldiers. From the very start, nitrate enmeshed documentary and fiction, the lived body and its objectification.

The complicit history of cinema and the military-industrial complex stretches from its very first materials and formations – such as the chronophotographic gun designed by Étienne-Jules Marey in 1882 – to contemporary 3D and immersive sound technologies, created with research and development funding from the US military. The Bolex camera and Nagra sound recorder – lightweight and affordable equipment that enabled the explosion of grassroots and *cinéma vérité* documentary, allied to civil rights and anti-colonial movements globally – were both developed to be robust and portable for use upon the battlefield by the US Army.

Among the first newsreels collected and distributed by the Pathé brothers were several that documented British troops in the Boer War at the turn of the century. Cinema's spectacular solicitation of its audience's attention was never just about technological wonder, but also fuelling racism and xenophobia. The earliest cameras were mobilised in the service of empire to feed what film scholar Fatimah Tobing Rony calls 'fascinating cannibalism', which she defines as white metropolitan audiences consuming colonised bodies, whose Othering was intensified by the camera that brought them, without their consent, into the visual field.

When we look at the newsreel image that Hirschfeld saw, we see an ambiguous figure. What we need to see is how it was framed: to see the way that Pathé and others indelibly shaped the visual field – what could be seen, and how it could be understood – while they simultaneously hid that framing through their presentation of objectivity.

We need to recognise not only what but how Pathé wanted us to see; to remember that, in producing this authoritative form of framing, they were contesting and silencing the lively, multifarious global modernisms that were staking their claim to the visual and other fields. We need to remember that the newsreel image had the effect of overwriting the cultures whose destruction it depicted. Watching newsreels that transport non-consenting bodies to voyeuristic audiences, what we see is decontextualized representations that enact a double erasure. Although it exploited the twenty-four-frames-per-second sensation of liveness that made motion pictures such a thrill, Pathé also participated in the vitrification of its living subjects.

It is an archive we were never supposed to see, no one here was supposed to live to see it.

Sho'ah images such as those of book-burnings, and the irreparable loss for which they stand, are a kind of double erasure: the documentation overwrites the meaning of what is documented while hiding what cannot be documented.

Jewish philosopher Jacques Derrida described the feeling of confronting such images as *mal d'archive* – typically translated as 'archive fever', a burning compulsion to engage with the fragmentary documentation as a way of recreating what is gone. I feel it is better expressed as 'archive ache': the phantom ache of the lost limb, the history that can be accessed only through its absence. This *mal* is a reminder of the precarity of the survival of marginalised communities. To call it an ache names the tension of doing work that appears to work against itself: to contain what can be found without demanding or inventing coherence; to embrace what has to be carried forward, but not uncritically; to bring together what needs to be connected without recourse to grand narratives or unifying theories.

Looked at in this way, the newsreel image disrupts persistence of vision: we see at once the existence of the books and papers, the work of the Institut für Sexualwissenschaft, including its immersion in colonial thought, *and* we see its almost complete and irreversible erasure.

Once seen, you cannot unsee the doubling and its implications. The archive captures the act of erasure *and* – and herein lies the aching possibility – a flaming trace of that which it tried to erase. Attending to the trace, the possibility, is the repeated work felt as an ache for what has been lost. A persistent ache can push you to stretch, and stretching can release deep feelings of grief and rage. These motivate an urgency to learn more and to continue the work in the present; and, in order to do so, to fold time so that there is - even if only imaginatively - *more* past work, *more* that was made and that survived in order to sustain us.

Setting itself against the imperative, folded time explores and values the subjunctive, a grammar of the speculative that cannot erase erasure, but can refuse its totality. It asks: what if Hirschfeld had been able to screen *Different From the Others* to fellow Parisian Jean Cocteau, the multimodal artist rejected by the Surrealist movement for being too queer, who made the homoerotic avant-garde film *The Blood of a Poet* (1930).

Scrapping around in the archive, I find evidence enough that the two may have at least known of each other to permit a subjunctive imagining. Cocteau's uncle Raymond, his mother's brother, was the first secretary to the French Embassy in Berlin, and was embroiled in the Eulenberg affair, in which the endemic blackmail of gay men under the Prussian civil code reached the inner circle of the German emperor Wilhelm, a scandal that eventually led to Raymond's suicide. Hirschfeld testified at the trial. Of his uncle, Cocteau only remembered a dramatic scene with his mother, a fragment: 'some sealed packets that were thrown onto the fire... nothing remains, alas!' Queerness is 'thrown onto the fire' in the family, as by the state. But the burning act of erasure provokes the young Jean's curiosity and remains burned into his imagination.

These Magic Eye moments of doubling, of seeing the irruptive imagination within the absolute destruction – of enunciating a subjunctive to stand against the imperative – sometimes seem like the only resistance to the erasive force intended by *entartet*.

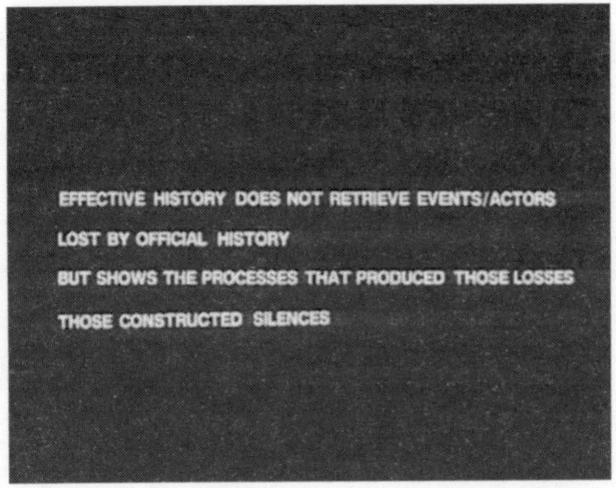

Researching QUILTBAG erasure in the archives, lesbian filmmaker Barbara Hammer found a trace in the most surprising place: classical Hollywood. Her research into early experimental X-ray photographer James Sibley Watson led her to another of his interventions into the visual field: the first American fiction feature with explicit gay content.

A silent black-and-white Biblical epic, *Lot in Sodom* was made in 1933 by Watson and Melville Webber, alongside a number of crew members who had fled Eastern Europe because they were queer or Jewish or both. The stylisation of the Sodomites in the film, sporting heavy guyliner, makes it apparent that, even for queer Jewish Europeans, there is a persistent characterisation of homosexuality as Other to Eurowestern society, and particularly as Orientalised. Another double vision: by locating queerness historically within the Biblical narrative, the film also dislocates it from American modernity, protecting itself from censorship.

In her 1992 experimental documentary *Nitrate Kisses*, her first feature-length film, Hammer takes up the fragments of *Lot in Sodom* and reads this ambiguous figure in all its QUILTBAG beauty and its racialised cliché.

In order to reframe them, Hammer intercuts *Lot in Sodom*'s stylised Biblical queers with her own footage of a mixed-race gay male couple having sex as the voiceover narrates *Lot*'s battle with the censors and the institution of the Motion Picture Production Code – a 'moral code' commissioned by Hollywood studios when, in 1922, they became nervous about the economic effect of high-profile off-screen sexual assault cases involving well-known actors. Presbyterian elder Will H. Hays, who was hired to rehabilitate the industry, adopted the 1930 code written by a film journalist and a Jesuit priest that came to be known by his name. The Hays Code forbids, among other things, depictions of both homosexuality – never mentioned in the code, but implicitly covered (or doubly erased) by the phrase 'sex perversion' – and interracial relationships. In *Nitrate Kisses*, the code is superimposed over a sequence of one partner's condom-clad penis gliding toward the camera across his partner's anus, literally fucking (up) the imposition of Christianised morality on cinema, while reinserting explicit sexuality into *Lot* and critiquing its racism.

Using a combination of archive footage, voiceover narration and live sex between diverse couples, Hammer's experimental film embeds the homophobic, racist policies of the Reagan and Bush administrations within the history of American censorship of queer bodies. It is a lot, because it had to be.

Nitrate Kisses emerged from the queer cultural revival that started in the 1970s, and became all the more urgent as it faced eradication by the impact of the Reagan administration's genocidal mishandling of AIDS, which created an epidemic. *Nitrate Kisses* offers a necessary pre-history of the way in which QUILTBAG people were being condemned to death by a negligent government – or, in the case of *Lot*, a malign God.

'It's about the status of strangers', says a voiceover speaker, referring to the story of Sodom. At the time of *Nitrate Kisses*, the word *status* is freighted with the double meaning of socio-economic ranking and of being HIV-positive or -negative. The film uses *Lot* to address the intersections between these meanings, how the US government's response to AIDS gave sufferers of the disease 'the status of strangers', at a time when 'strangers' – immigrants, dissidents, Black and Indigenous people, feminists, trans people, queers – were avowedly unwelcome in American social politics.

The final sections of *Nitrate Kisses* turn to erasing the erasure of lesbians within the history of Nazi persecution, drawing on police records, archival fragments and oral history, which Hammer supplements with a contemporary lesbian BDSM scene. When one voiceover speaker mentions 'oral history', there is a swift, funny and knowing cut to oral sex between the couple.

One intervention into the erasive state archive is to make the lived body – especially the body classed as deviant because it is sexual, and because it is not cis male – palpable. Diana Taylor calls this 'the repertoire': forms of irruptive, excessive – often oral – performance and embodied memory that cannot be captured by the records. Attending to performance works by contemporary Indigenous artists in the Americas, and forms of protest such as Las Madres de la Plaza de Mayo, Taylor argues that the body is both itself a record and a technology of transmission, which can be wielded by those excluded by colonialism and heteropatriarchy *because* it is devalued and made invisible. Its liveness eludes fixity and refuses atomisation: like Hirschfeld's vision of desire, it is necessarily connective and therefore potentially revolutionary.

Nitrate Kisses puts the kisses back onto nitrate, exploding the myth of a monolithically heteronormative cinema by reimagining the film that almost existed within the imaginary of the film that was almost lost. A film that could never have been made. It is a film that queers the cinematic by contesting the objective status of documentary, opening it up to include the imaginary, the erotic, the complex, and the diverse - everything that Pathé pushed so hard to exclude.

I didn't see Hammer's film when it first toured the feminist and queer festival circuit in the early 1990s, thanks to two forms of censorship. First because the British Board of Film Classification defined me as too young to know my own history, and, beyond that, because of Section 28, a 1988 amendment to the Local Government Act that censored the 'promotion' of queer culture, thus denying me access to knowledge of the existence of either the film or the festivals.

But it was because of those festivals that I was, eventually, able to see it. Those festivals generate a persistence of vision by continuing to screen Hammer's work, something in which I participate as a queer feminist film curator. Independent QUILTBAG and feminist festivals, distributors, critics, scholars, publishers, funders and arts activists have enabled filmmakers to disrupt generational patterns of erasure, making precariously visible what was once completely hidden.

Nitrate Kisses changed our present, which was its future, by changing the past. It's a queer strategy of folding time, one that it shared with a whole cohort of films travelling the same circuits, looping around and in conversation with each other through their queer activation of archive materials. The film closest to *Nitrate Kisses* is Black British artist-filmmaker Isaac Julien's *Looking for Langston* (1989), made around the time of the implementation of Section 28, just as I was coming to queer consciousness. Looking for a history of himself, Julien imagined the Harlem Renaissance poet Langston Hughes through a series of scenes including a delirious dance party choreographed by desire that fuses the besuited jazz club speakeasies of the 1920s with their descendants, 1980s discos and drag balls.

It is a Black flourishing, a beating heart of global modernisms that continues to inspire subjunctive imaginings - not because of its visibility, but its attempted erasure. Julien faced the very censorship he challenged. The Hughes family estate refused him permission to quote from the poet, maintaining that the film was libellous.

When Saidiya Hartman takes up images of Black fin-de-siècle lives in New York and Philadelphia in her 2019 book *Wayward Lives, Beautiful Experiments*, she uses repertoire in a way similar to Julien's 1920s ball to prise them from the official archives. Her subjects are the 'riotous Black girls, troublesome women and queer radicals' whose lives can often only be traced through the systemically racist criminal justice system and the writings of sociologists that supported it. Folded within court and newspaper records of abusive correctional facilities, and within the documentation of white landladies, Hartman also finds the few letters, diaries, snapshots and oral histories which were preserved as condemnatory evidence. Reframing this material, Hartman allows us to hear, instead, a condemnation of those who incarcerated and judged.

Like Julien, Hartman makes singing, dancing, queer interstitial spaces – from rent parties to uptown lesbian orgies – central to her argument. Active, public, vivid, polymorphous sexuality, she argues, is fundamental to modernity and modernisms, and it was 'riotous' urban Black womxn and queers who pioneered it. She reframes the photographs and fragmentary accounts that she finds not only as anti-carceral abolitionism, but equally as a new and vital account of modernity told through the motion and embodied knowledge of Black dancers, musicians, sex workers, girlfriends, artists and friends.

Dig if you will the picture, Hartman urges, imagining a film starring blues singer Gladys Bentley as (a version of) himself, assigning Bentley the pronoun that best describes his suit-wearing, bulldagger swagger.

Hartman presses her imaginary film, *Mistah Beauty*, into the canon of Oscar Micheaux, likely the most prolific independent filmmaker in early American cinema, who wrote, produced and directed forty-four feature-length films between 1919 and 1948. Micheaux's achievement is almost hallucinatory in itself, not only because his parents had been enslaved, but because his work was brutally neglected for nearly forty years, until African-American film historians such as Pearl Bowser began to recover and recontextualise it.

Only three of Micheaux's silents, and five of his sound features, survive. It is the survival of these eight films that makes Hartman's imaginative insertion into Micheaux's oeuvre possible; it is the erasure of those that were lost that makes it necessary.

Her imagined film brings vividly to life the Jazz Age which Bentley celebrated and helped create. Jazz travelled in the bodies of its performers who played and lived in Europe, as well as on wax cylinder and film, indelibly shaping the queerness of Weimar culture and cinema. *Mistah Beauty* calls attention to another erasure: the absence of African-American repertoire in the archiving of the European queer cultures to which it gave life and form.

Hartman's subjunctive scenario shows that,

although Taylor considers them an oppositional binary, the repertoire is always subversively present in the archive, disrupting it from within, creating what I term an 'anarchive'. In recording the facts of bodies and lives, of the cultures it is trying to suppress and destroy, the archive always undermines itself and its claims to stability and totality. Any archive is subverted into the anarchive: the embodied power of the moving bodies it attempts to disembody, the organic and communitarian knowledge and art practices it attempts to rubbish and suppress. Archiving and classifying, as acts of domination, speak of their fear of what they are trying to contain. The anarchive is the record of that uncontainability.

Criminalisation inheres in the concept of *entartung*. Nordau dedicated *Degeneration* to Cesare Lombroso, the founder of criminal anthropology, who argued that 'crime' inheres in the body, that it is hereditary and that it is expressed through visible physical traits. Lombroso turned to photography, a cutting-edge technology in 1860, to create his still-influential taxonomical portraits of 'criminals'. While we rightly dismiss phrenology as ridiculous, often we forget the complicit role that photography played in the development of the theory of a legible physiognomy; that it was embraced because of a belief that the body exhibited (degenerate) character traits which it could capture and make available to categorisation.

KwaZulu South African visual activist Zanele Muholi turns Lombroso's techniques back on themselves. *Faces and Phases 2006–14* is a series of large, black-and-white photographic portraits, arranged in a grid deliberately reminiscent of a 'Wanted' gallery. The portraits have been made in collaboration with their subjects: lesbians, gender non-conforming womxn and trans men who have faced and survived the brutally misnamed practice of 'curative' rape in South Africa. In these enlivening, unruly portraits, the subjects stare into camera, resisting the fixity of the criminalising arrest image. Facing forwards, in defiance, they stare down any idea that their identity is criminal; that it is fixed – or fixable – by others.

The portraits, in all their autonomous variety rooted in a continuity with precolonial QUILTBAG identities, stand together collectively, refusing both the homogenisation of the type and the isolation of the mug shot. Muholi's portraits make visible how contemporary attacks on QUILTBAG communities perpetuate colonial-era laws and violence, including in South Africa; an archive the British government continues to suppress. The Nazis were openly influenced by Britain's invention of concentration camps at the end of the Second Boer War, in which more than 100,000 indigenous people were interned, as were about 120,000 Boer settlers (kept in less degrading conditions) who were classified as enemy combatants.

Newsreel operates on the assumption that what is documented cannot be forgotten or unseen. What newsreel records is forgotten because it is not held in collective memory. Muholi articulates how their work speaks with a continuous collective presence, folding time through their non-binary pronoun. 'I say "they" as in my ancestors, and even deeper than that. The collective.'

If we're going to look in on *entartet*, we need the complex, collective, enfolded sensibilities of queer *sexualwissenschaft* in order to read it.

I mean read in the sense defined, performed and handed down by Dorian Corey, mother of the House of Corey, as recorded in the legendary - and controversial - documentary *Paris is Burning* (Jennie Livingston, 1990). Even on its release, critics such as bell hooks queried its relation to the 'fascinating cannibalism' of anthropological film and the related economic exploitation of its subjects. In acknowledgement, I want to centre the authorship of the ball culture performers who speak the film's truths, listening in on their queer theorising through the rest of this essay.

This is how Dorian describes the genesis of reading as a practice within ball culture:

> Shade comes from reading. Reading came first. Reading is the real art form

> of insult... You found a flaw and exaggerated it, then you've got a good read going.

Muholi's portraits, like Hartman's and Hammer's revisions, are 'reads' in this sense. They draw attention to the flawed frame of Eurowestern dominant culture and push against it. Rather than centring erasure, they foreground the unruly, persistent, sexual body that enables us to understand what we are seeing.

This emphasis is also exactly at the heart of Hirschfeld's *sexualwissenschaft*, the German term for sexology. *Wissenschaft* is usually translated as science, but its meaning is much broader, encompassing any systematic research, or body of knowledge gathered through observation.

Unlike sexology, *sexualwissenschaft* – looked at again – could mean something like sexuality as a way of doing research; even, prefiguring the work of Michel Foucault, sexuality as an epistemology, a way of knowing. *Sexualwissenschaft* may have combined sociology, psychology, philology, archaeology and literary criticism to do cultural history, but it did so primarily through the repertoire: the lived experience of sexual and gender dissidence.

We have to read against the work done by *entartet*, read to recover from it, read to condemn it by clarifying its lies. If we as queers are here, then we are here to *read*: to contest official accounts. Queer and trans Black and Latinx ballroom culture teaches us to read those histories, to use our *sexualwissenschaft*. As Dorian exhorts, we need to continue to throw shade; to find the flaws in the official histories and exaggerate them for all to see, because it is official histories that have been involved in what *Paris is Burning*'s speakers describe as 'passing'. They mean passing, for reasons of safety and security, as white, straight, middle class and/or gender conforming. However, we need to look, instead, at how dominant cultures and official histories 'pass'

– as objective, unassailable and totalising – as part of their violently erasive operations.

It is easier to treat Nazi ideology and practices as *entartet* – as outside the set of all sets of human behaviour – than to see them as part of a shared history. Framing Nazi ideology as not just an exception but *the* exception conforms to the Pathé version of history, the single story that exempts us from complicity. It unfolds time by rendering Nazi fascism as a fixed point that neither extends back through colonial histories nor forward into contemporary authoritarian populisms that take their shape from such erasures of historical continuity and memory.

'Colonialism is one variety of fascism', as the Tunisian-Jewish radical anti-colonial writer Albert Memmi famously said. Like other fascisms, colonialism proudly staged its own acts of whitewashing as self-advertisements like *Entartete 'Kunst'*. In her book *Imperial Leather* (1995), the feminist historian Anne McClintock reads Victorian advertisements for domestic and bodily cleaning products as an archive of racism: products that scrubbed away any trace of embodiment, while also wiping out the Black women on whose labour the world depended. History and lived experience are whitewashed, and colonial 'cleanliness' is sold in order to shame. One of the most powerful tools that connects colonialism and fascism is shame. Shame – accompanied by the mechanisms and metaphors of 'cleaning' – undergird how *entartet* does its erasive work.

In *As We Have Always Done*, Anishinaabe scholar and poet Leanne Betasamosake Simpson describes how shame was and continues to be used to undermine Indigenous cultures – and how Indigenous *sexualwissenschaft* 'reads' settler texts to undermine their cis heteronormativity right back. She describes how colonial missionaries targeted the 'grounded normativity' – the everydayness – of gender and sexual diversity in the First Nations they encountered, as a deliberate method for destroying communities and cultures. In their writings, missionaries salivated over the lack of (unnecessary) clothing, the apparent disorganisation and plurality of sexual relations (which followed rigorous codes of respect, just not hierarchized or churched ones), and likewise the apparent disregard for a fixed gender binary in all aspects of life. Then – because the practices they had fetishized called into question the entire missionizing project – they targeted them for eradication.

These writings are often the only archives that remain of precolonial gendered and sexual lifeways. Simpson notes that, in his 'captivity' narrative, John Tanner, a white settler who was raised by an Ottawa woman, uses the term *agokwa*, with reference to a Two-Spirit/Queer Ojibwe warrior named Ozawendib, to denote a male-bodied person who had husbands and was addressed by the pronoun 'she'. In recent years, Two Spirit/Queer First Nations artists such as Cree painter and performance artist Kent Monkman and Plains Cree filmmaker Thirza Cuthand have prised the evidence available within these unreliable reports, re-appropriating and recontextualising it through surviving languages, stories and traditions. They have pieced together a QUILTBAG no longer framed by Tanner's pejorative claim that Ozawendib's place in her community was 'disgusting'.

Similarly, Muholi's recent self-portrait series *Somnyama Ngonyama, Hail the Dark Lioness* refuses colonial disgust by embracing that which has been termed disgusting: specifically, the objects associated with the labour and bodies McClintock identifies as being erased. Taking up the physical reminders of their mother's work as a cleaner, Muholi creates ritual costumes from domestic objects such as laundry pegs, vacuum cleaner tubes and rubber gloves. This refuses any sharp separation between the acceptable and the unacceptable, the historical and the contemporary, the decorative and the political, or the domestic and the magical. Instead, these objects, as ritual costume, are immanent, connected, contestatory.

When Muholi wears the world that they carry in their body, they embrace their mother's skilled domestic work as itself an artistic practice. You cannot see these portraits except in their specificity and with their evocation of a long tradition. The QUILTBAG's crafty origins, its practical spirituality, its care and its carefulness, manifest as a riposte to the homogenising, categorising colonial archive and gaze.

It is a photograph that no one wants to see, but not in the sense that was intended.

Entartete 'Kunst' was an attempt to whitewash what was seen as shameful dirt: the Nazi in Opernplatz throws the books so vehemently surely because he is trying to pass, to dispose of a part of himself.

That tens of thousands of people attended *Entartete 'Kunst'* feels like a similar vehemence, a forceful gesture of rejection. Yet putting so much energy into rejecting something that is literally named *entartet* – nothing, outside all comprehension or value – is telling. A decade earlier, Sigmund Freud threw shade on exactly this kind of over-investment in refusal, arguing that it points to a powerful act of whitewashing: what is being negated is being sanitised, making it assimilable so long as the threat of its tempting, freeing lifeforce is completely deadened. 'Negation's "no"', he writes, 'is the hall-mark of repression, a certificate of origin – like, let us say, "Made in Germany."' Writing in 1925, Freud slyly identifies a hallmark of pre-war German culture, what could be called its reprussian; it's a prescient observation about the forces of negation that will explode after and against Weimar. By attending *Entartete 'Kunst'* and rejecting its degenerate artworks, viewers sought, through a public act of negation, to be certified as 'Made in Germany'.

Beneath that frisson, however, is a deeper 'no': the way the Nazis repeatedly drew upon the repressive potential of representation already present in the museum space, the documentary photograph and the film that had already quashed liveness and liveliness. Their insistent, leaden literalness was totalising, admitting no reads – so much so that they made an exhibition of themselves.

Opposite the vast, chaotic exhibition of modernist artworks they titled *Entartete 'Kunst'*, the Nazis also created a similarly revealing monument to themselves, a showcase of their vision of the visual arts of the Fatherland in all their woodenly muscular verisimilitude. *The Great German Art Exhibition*, named for its intention to make German art great again, was also exhibited in Munich in 1937. Unlike the modernist exhibition, however, it was spread across acres of white space in a purpose-built gallery personally funded by Hitler. Lacking the imaginative flair to be accidentally camp, the Fatherland's stultifying propaganda drew a tiny, dutiful audience compared to the astounding number of visitors that attended the *Entartete 'Kunst'* show.

It is a painting we never saw, because we are ashamed.

A better clue to the function of the *Entartete 'Kunst'* exhibition lies in its grassroots precursors, the *Schandausstellungen*: literally, exhibitions of shame. These exhibitions were organised by local supporters of the Nazi-allied *Kampfbund für Deutsche Kultur* in 1933, as takeovers of museums whose curators were classified as Weimar loyalists. A shame-exhibition in Mannheim used the term 'cultural Bolshevism'

– an anti-Semitic dog-whistle, one still popular with contemporary right-wing media – to refer to art by *Neue Sachlichkeit* and Expressionist artists.

The *Schandausstellungen* intended to cast shame on the former curators of the museums, who were often ousted, on the artists and their patrons, but also on any viewer who had previously admired or responded positively or curiously to such artworks. For the unrepressed individuals and communities allied to Weimar, the *Schandaustellungen* acted like public shamings that required citizens to declare loyalty to the new regime of negation or else risk being labelled *entartet*. Like *Entartete 'Kunst'* a few years later, *Schandausstellungen* used pre-existing practices of hyper-visibility in order to foreclose any shame that audiences might experience in looking at 'pornographic' and 'disgusting' modern art, given the decades of *entartung* propaganda. Not so much an exhibition, as exhibitionism: shame was extracted from the viewers by inviting them to heap it upon the work, in its very visibility. This method drew on the longstanding voyeuristic function of Eurowestern circuses and freak shows; of psychiatric institutions like the Salpêtrière, where Nordau's mentor Jean-Martin Charcot had his female hysterics perform their symptoms for his contemporaries and students, including Freud; and even queer Berlin *kabaretts*, where tourists were welcome. Twenty years before *Entartete 'Kunst'*, Berliners attended human zoos in prisoner-of-war camps, where captured soldiers who had served (and were done the disservice of being ranked second-class) in the Allies' African, Asian and First Nations troops were exhibited and examined under the guise of anthropological 'education'.

From their very beginnings, anthropology and evolutionary science are, as Banu Subramaniam argues, 'fascinating cannibalism', held captive in the frame of Enlightenment values, in which imperial economics always outranks liberation.

Enlightenment practices such as the scientific method and documentary do not describe reality, but circumscribe it. As an unidentified speaker says outside one of the balls, which infused the long history of Harlem nightlife with the costuming and walking of New Orleans Mardi Gras parades, in *Paris is Burning*:

> You go in there and you feel... you feel a hundred percent right as being gay... It's not what it's like in the world. It's not what it's like in the world. You know, it should be like that in the world.

Sexualwissenschaft is a way of knowing how it should be. For Hirschfeld (and for the early Freud, before he denied his previous alignment with socialism in order to assimilate psychoanalysis and refute the anti-Semitic charges against it), fully-realised embodiment was the root of revolution.

Hirschfeld had famously used sexuality and sexology to critique the damaging repressions caused by Prussian machismo in his magnum opus *The Sexual History of the World War.*

Documenting the homoeroticism of military training, the significant role of sex workers in maintaining front-line morale, psychosexual impairments in veterans, and the empowerment of women through nursing, intelligence and other war work, Hirschfeld made the opposite argument to Nordau's claims that European masculinity proved its virility on the battlefield. Thinking about gender and sexuality through militarism, Hirschfeld demonstrated that they were not fixed but contextual, and that gender non-conforming behaviours threatened imperialist rhetoric by revealing the world as it should be. In his hands, *sexualwissenschaft* was, as it remains, powerful, radical and dangerous, which is why the Nazis were so furiously determined to erase it.

They had to try and remove queer and trans knowledge and activism from its central situation in the political and artistic whirl that made up Weimar Berlin's challenges to imperial, Prussian Germany, and the role that its dissidence could play in the broader continuum of anti-fascist politics. It was imperative for the Nazis to place *sexualwissenschaft*, which foregrounded the knowledge and continuous histories of queer and trans people, among the 'un-German' forms of knowledge, and ways of being, they set out to destroy.

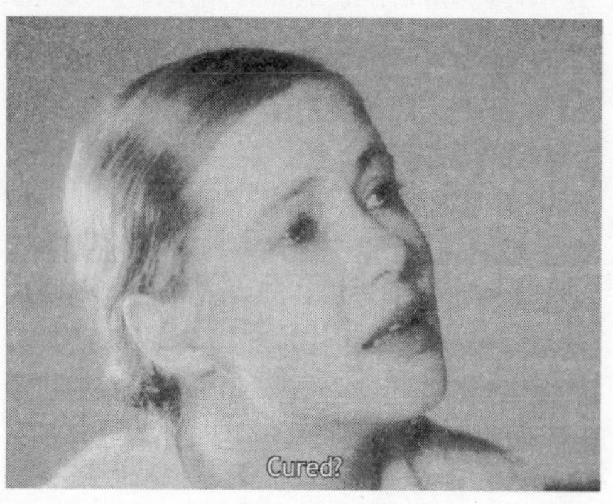

It is a scene we never saw, even as we were seeing it.

With their extensive destruction of queer culture, and subsequent selective preservation with *Entartete 'Kunst'*, the Nazis made a *schandausttellung* of *sexualwissenschaft*. They decontextualized the fragments of Weimar queer culture that have survived.

Preservation pins the traces of a 'lost' history in museum conditions, disconnected from their milieu where lived experience and political resistance were inextricable. When these traces become archival objects they are separated out from a living artistic culture. 'Different from the others', these creative works are only permitted to exist as historical documents. Their visibility amid scarcity creates an ambiguous image, where it's hard not to see them as evidence of loss, rather than engage with the fullness of their presence.

After the war, the 1931 film *Mädchen in Uni-*

form became known as 'anti-authoritarian and prophetically anti-fascist' for its depiction of open resistance in a Prussian girls' school ('known' by reputation, because most of the prints were purged by the Nazis). Yet, as B. Ruby Rich argues, this undeniably accurate designation strips the film of its complexity, wherein resistance emerges directly from the students' anti-patriarchal queer lived experience and the public recognition of private desire.

The uniform of the title makes a parallel between the repressive discipline of the all-girl's school, producing obedient imperial subjects, and the equally same-sex world of the army: in the opening minute, there's a cut from soldiers marching in the street to schoolgirls walking in a cloister. It is, in fact, when the protagonist Manuela crosses the sartorial gender binary that what is considered a schoolgirl crush – *schwarmerei* – becomes fully realised desire. For the film's central scene, she is cast as the lead in Friedrich Schiller's play *Don Carlos*, which is staged in the gymnasium for the headmistress's birthday. She gives a thrilling performance in the breeches role of the young prince who falls in love with his step-mother, queering a canonical German text. Fräulein von Bernburg, the teacher with whom Manuela is in love, watches silently from the front row, leaning forward. 'But the way she looked at you, you can't imagine', another girl tells Manuela after the play. At the after-party, a drunk Manuela announces her love to her fellow students, which is no secret as all the girls have a crush on the kind, young von Bernburg. More radically, she asserts, 'I know she loves me.' When the forbidding headmistress enters the party, Manuela shouts, 'She loves me. I fear nothing.'

In the school infirmary, where Manuela is isolated after she faints, the headmistress three times uses the word *Schande*, shame, to describe Manuela's actions. 'People like you are banned from society', she threatens. But it is the headmistress who will be banned, driven away when Manuela's classmates, aided by von Bernburg, rescue her from an attempted suicide. 'Because I can't bear for her to suffer injustice', von Bernburg declares passionately to the French teacher who tries to stop her ruining her career. *Sexualwissenschaft* is solidarity.

At the start of her memoir, Marlene Dietrich – who left Berlin for Los Angeles in 1930 – tells a story about her own schooldays that connects her stand against Nazism in her war work, her career as an international performer, and (implicitly) her bisexuality. Her childhood memory of the Great War is defined by the brutal dismissal of her gymnasium's French teacher (as an enemy alien), who taught her to read poetry aloud and on whom she had a crush. Dietrich's trouser- (and occasionally tux-) wearing films in Hollywood with Josef von Sternberg were better-known than *Mädchen*. Read, even at the time, as implicitly queer, their coded subtlety and skewed family values allowed them to pass as Dietrich herself did.

Mädchen is considered the first film to feature an openly lesbian protagonist. It is also the first fiction feature by a German-speaking woman director, Leontine Sagan, who was of Jewish descent. Sagan's sexuality, like Dietrich's, is the source of much speculation, but she moved in the queer milieux of Weimar, and then London's West End theatre scene, where she worked with out gay composer Ivor Novello. Sagan never made another lesbian film.

It was precisely the way in which *Mädchen*, part of the larger vivid experimental cinema of German Expressionism, entwined explicit sexuality and radical politics that made it the target of Nazism. Censorship and eradication cut down an emerging queer cinema as it found its form. Just as it was being developed, cinema's potential to express *sexualwissenschaft*, as an art form of the desired and autonomous body, was brutally cancelled out.

One of the most valuable aspects of *Mädchen in Uniform* is that it exists; its international success outside Germany enabled Sagan to leave and survive, and pursue an émigré career across the arts that included becoming the first female producer at London's Drury Lane Theatre. The film's survival, even in rare prints – even in rumour – also came to act as evidence for queer pre-war lives and cinema, and stands at the root of the evolution of queer film discourse.

Mädchen is metonymic of Weimar queer culture: its unprecedented boldness and openness made possible its circulation and the deep impression it made on viewers (it inspired one of the first queer youth fandoms, the Romanian 'longstockings and kissing' cult) that led to its cultural survival; likewise, that deep impression condemned it to censorship and attempted erasure. Yet censorship and erasure themselves act as a kind of archive, particularly given the Nazis' obsessional attention to self-documentation. As noted in Alain Resnais' documentary *Night and Fog* (1956), via the voiceover written by Chris Marker and Jean Cayrol, the Nazis documented their activities with every tool available because they believed they had right on their side. They were keen adopters of lightweight film cameras, and Resnais excerpts some of their footage in his film, one of the first cinematic reflections on the Holocaust.

Not only does Resnais' film assert, categorically, that there is nothing inherently radical about the act of filmmaking itself, but it considers very carefully the nature of visibility. The film's footage of Auschwitz ends with a watchtower. The camera, suggests Resnais, was similarly wielded as a death machine. Not only were the Nazis documenting their own actions approvingly, but through the camera they were erasing peoples and cultures by documenting them; by capturing them, rendering them obsolete objects for an Archaeological Institute display.

That you can watch thousands of hours of

Nazi film footage pays tribute to the intensely difficult work of historians, archivists, restorers, filmmakers and scholars who have preserved documentation in the face of Holocaust denial. They have turned an archive intended to valorise and validate genocide into its opposite: a way to counter erasure, or at least to make it palpable; and even make palpable the absence of a counter-archive. Absolute control of the visual field means eliminating anything that might disrupt or contest it.

It is a film no one here can see, because no one had the chance to make it.

Occasionally, the archive holds the trace of a trace that sparks both imagination and rage: what if this film had existed? Specifically, what if radical Soviet filmmaker Sergei Eisenstein, himself of Jewish descent, had been able to talk to Magnus Hirschfeld when he came to Berlin for that express purpose? Eisenstein was returning from shooting footage for *¡Qué viva México!* in 1930 (although a feature-length version of the film would not be released until 1979). Shooting the film had such an intense impact on his sexual and gender identity that he not only wrote to Hirschfeld, but followed up his (unanswered) letter with an unannounced visit. Eisenstein sought approval and acceptance for his theory that the artistic self is androgynous (as Virginia Woolf also famously thought), or what he called bisexual, a word that, for him, blended genderqueerness and queer desire.

In fact, Eisenstein conceptualised and pursued bisexuality in a Hegelian sense: the synthesis of thesis and antithesis. He did so not only as evidence that G. W. F. Hegel was bisexual (his evidence for which forms an extensive section of his letter to Hirschfeld), but also as inspired by and exactly equivalent to Karl Marx's use of the dialectic as the engine of political revolution. For Eisenstein, a bisexual synthesis was a radically political transformation of human sexuality and society.

To recognise this project, the most radical filmmaker of the interwar era sought out its most radical social scientist. Perhaps it was Eisenstein who had brought that wayward copy of Hirschfeld's documentary *Laws of Love* to Moscow, curious to see the radical scientist speaking in his, Eisenstein's, cinematic language. The film's vocabulary of animal sexual diversity may have informed Eisenstein's little-known multispecies erotic drawings, which were exhibited in New York in 2017.

Eisenstein's radicalism inhered in his belief that cultural instances – not so much texts themselves, but rather our interactions with them – could change us; could radicalise our politics. Much as Hirschfeld saw the potential role of sexuality in post-war revolutions, so Eisenstein saw the cinematic relations between viewer and image, effected by the radical encounter between two disparate images. He called this encounter 'montage', a French word that literally means mounting; his erotic drawings, annotated in French, suggest he was well aware of the double entendre. Eisenstein's images shock as they fuck each other across the frame. Montage arouses us; while plenty of attention has been given to its ability to awaken us critically to rise up, the role of its erotic charge in calling us to action has been ignored, unseen and unwanted. Speculating about the montage of Eisenstein and Hirschfeld changes the frame – which is, after all, what Eisenstein himself was aiming to do.

In creating juxtapositions that called for interpretation, rather than smoothing out sense across the cut, he pre-empted a later sexual politics of cinema, in which feminists rejected what they called 'suture', the way that traditional Hollywood editing stitches the viewer into the world of the mainstream narrative film so that we are uncritical of the politics it is propagandising: capitalist, colonialist, cisheteronormative. Feminist filmmakers went back to ideas such as Eisenstein's to formulate a radical counter-cinema of refusal, unsmoothing the narrative seams and even ripping them apart. Trans film theorist Susan Stryker takes the point further when she argues that the 'transsexual body... presents critical opportunities similar to those offered by the camera', and even more so by montage, in the way that it makes 'visible the culturally specific mechanisms of achieving gendered embodiment.' Cinema and bodies (can) imagine each other's radical potential.

It is an insight Eisenstein never articulated explicitly in his cinematic or theoretical oeuvre: it remained imagined in his bottom drawer drawings, and in his longing letter to a potential collaborator. But when Eisenstein, aroused by Mexico, arrived in Berlin, Hirschfeld was on an international speaking tour that would become permanent exile. Eisenstein returned to the USSR, his needs unmet.

It is almost physically painful to confront the absence of the *sexualwissenschaft* cinema that Eisenstein might have made with a sympathetic community in Berlin. Only a couple of years previously, while touring western Europe in 1929, he supervised the making of a Swiss educational documentary about abortion titled *Frauennot – Frauenglück* (*Women's Misery, Women's Happiness*).

Eisenstein was concerned not just with a cinema that showed characters who were 'different from others', but a cinema of difference.

It was a film he made but no one ever talks about.

It would be nearly fifty years after Hirschfeld's death before a filmmaker would come close to realising that lost film, and few people have had the chance to see it. *Imagining October* (1984), a film by Derek Jarman.

In Jarman's book about filmmaking and family *The Last of England* (reprinted as *Kicking the Pricks*, his preferred original title), he describes the incendiary experience of a ten-day trip to the USSR in October 1984, with a number of other British independent filmmakers, to fulfil the request that he make a short film to be screened at the London Film Festival on his return. Having smuggled in Super-8 cassettes (as well as condoms), he walked through Moscow, filming the moment just before perestroika in the streets – and also in the Eisenstein Museum, housed in and preserving the filmmaker's apartment. In Baku, where Jarman filmed the eternal flame in a Zoroastrian monastery, a promised screening of his *Tempest* (1979) never materialised; he and fellow radical Sally Potter had caused an upset in Moscow by talking publicly about feminism and sexual dissidence.

On his return to London, he cut together a twenty-seven-minute film which draws parallels between the marketplace censorship that he, along with other queer and experimental artists, experienced in Thatcherite Britain, and the more manifest repression within the USSR. The film montages avant-garde works – partial, fragmentary, ironic, contested, self-mocking and raw – with state monuments, which Jarman says he found dangerously erotic, because of the seduction of their insistence on perfection.

Jarman titled the film *Imagining October*, in reference to Eisenstein's film *October: Ten Days that Shook the World* (1928), made to mark the tenth anniversary of the Russian Revolution.

I have seen *Imagining October* only once, and

both the film and the opportunity were so overwhelming that it is hard to reconstruct. I have to imagine it by turning to Jarman's diaries and published scripts – just as *Different From the Others* survived as a trace, through its printed scenarios and reviews. Encountering difficult-to-impossible to see QUILTBAG films through written texts creates another wave of temporal and affective folding, especially as even relatively recent films are subject to wilful neglect: if they are seen in their moment, they must be remanded in it. Acquired as museum pieces, they are either assigned to dusty storerooms, or canonised in order to be beyond reach.

Although it is not a monumental film, *Blue* – Jarman's last film, made in 1993, initially for live performance, when he was in the late stages of AIDS-related illnesses – has come to monumentalise him, and to monumentalise the self-congratulatory tolerance of assimilative forms of homonationalism represented by David Cameron's claim, on leaving office the day after the Brexit referendum, that at least he had legalised same-sex marriage.

Blue is a daring swoon of a film, a challenge and an assertion as fabulous as drag. But it has been positioned as a monument that is at once a memorial to an individual, and (against its intention) a celebration of the 'progressive' state and institutions which never supported the filmmaker while he was alive. When it is pinned in the gallery, no one has to listen to the formidable soundtrack, only drift past the lightbox-like screen. In being only seen within that frame – without its context, including knowledge of the liveness of its original performance – the film's power is diminished and contained.

The only canonisation Jarman accepted was that performed by drag nun AIDS activists the Sisters of Perpetual Indulgence, in Dungeness on 22 September 1991. They performed a benediction in Polari, which Paul Baker calls 'Britain's secret gay language', that made him the Sisters' first saint, St Derek of the Order of Celluloid Knights of Dungeness. Jarman received his title dressed in a robe designed by Sandy Powell for his film *Edward II* (1991) in which the Sisters appear as protestors. Together with the tall throne placed in his garden, the robe recalls Eisenstein's *Ivan the Terrible* (1944). Looking at Ed Sykes' black-and-white photograph of Jarman in his glittering robe on the shingle, I see Jarman outing Eisenstein, embodying his queerness, and the queerness of the radical energies of the Russian Revolution.

In Jarman's 1992 *Queer* series of paintings, polemic declarations – mostly single words and phrases – are graffitied (*sgraffito* means scratching, incising) into impasto oil paint layered over photocopies of British tabloid front pages. In 'Letter to the Minister', the backdrop is thirty-five photocopies, arranged in a 5x7 grid, of the infamously homophobic front page of the *Sun* from 1986. Headlined 'Vile Book in School', the lead article attacked Susanne Bosche's 1983 children's book *Jenny Lives with Eric and Martin*, and it became the catalyst for the introduction of Section 28 two years later.

Jarman's letter, beginning 'Dear William Shakespeare', is written as if from the fourteen-year-old Jarman, on discovering his condemned queerness at school. It lists the inspirations he would gather, his genealogy as a queer artist: famous historical figures whose sexuality has been suppressed, such as Shakespeare himself and Leonardo da Vinci. 'If I make films', the letter ends, 'I will make them like Eisenstein, Murnau, Pasolini, Visconti.'

It is a political declaration, a reminder that Jarman supported the revolutionary ideals of Soviet Communism as well as their radical expression in visual arts. Practising political aesthetics from first to last, Jarman prophetically refuses our contemporary situation, in which queer artists have come to be celebrated in a way that depoliticises sexuality into an assimilable neoliberal commodity, stripped of any revolutionary political force.

Signal artists are forced into a spotlight that essentialises their work: Vivek Shraya has named this demand 'trauma clowning', in an essay and accompanying photo series where she calls on decolonial QUILTBAG artists to push back against being tokenised by and for their decontextualized trauma. As Helen Charman writes about the erasure of the poet Denise Riley's socialist feminism, her 'work is heralded as radical, but only in relation to its softness.'

There is nothing soft or tragicizing about 'Letter to the Minister', which states above its epistolary text: 'Copies sent to the Arts Minister'; that is, to David Mellor, whose extra-marital affair was being revealed in the *Sun* exactly as Jarman's exhibition opened in Rome in July 1992. 'Tears fall behind the headlines', Jarman writes in the introduction to the catalogue for the exhibition. But he ends with the injunction: 'Don't cry over these works.' He describes rediscovering his youthful joy in painting large canvases, and also describes what stopped him painting.

'Find out who you really are, they said at

school', he writes in the introduction. 'What I discovered seemed terrible to me. Has sex ever been safe for me?' Folded time is not soft; it cannot soften the erasures and their terror. It can only resist them by insisting we face them. Jarman hands his teenage self a gift: not a letter *to*, assuming naïveté, but a recognition of the possibility of a letter *by*. He sees what was already present but latent at fourteen because it was repressed, and he sees how that presence, and the repression, fires him to resistance at fifty.

I was fifteen when I first saw Jarman's work. *Blue* was screened defiantly on Channel 4 on 19 September 1993, the startle of a silent blue screen that appeared long after the watershed at 10.45 pm; the soundtrack was played on BBC Radio 3. I didn't know how to read it: it read me. It taught me how to read for what was absent in my own life: the world as it should be. Jarman's work led me indirectly to Eisenstein, to Hirschfeld, to Hammer, to Muholi; to write this book as a letter not to but from my fifteen-year-old self, watching *Blue* in gratitude and grief and bewilderment. Aching.

Before the late 1970s, before Jarman and Isaac Julien – who in 2008 would make *Derek* about his friend's life, anarchivally placing live, performing bodies in the stillness of the BFI Archives – there was barely a British QUILTBAG cinema to speak of. The British queer wave came late to the screen, the foam at the end of a long European roller that formed in the immediate aftermath of WWII but did not crash into our closed island shores until the late 1970s. It is a cinema that begins in the ruins of the fascist powers and addresses their fascism head-on at a time when other artists were focused on reconstruction, or were practising ignorance.

Jarman's closest continental parallel is a Spanish filmmaker who faced down, survived and continues to reflect on the longest-lasting fascist regime in Europe; who, in the last days of Franco, made films that shouted 'Fuck me, fuck me, fuck me'.

Like Jarman, Pedro Almódovar – who kick-started his career with a short film of that title – was immersed within a counterculture of punk bands and graffiti artists. Associated with La Movida Madrileña, he translated that scene's DIY energy and confrontational attitude to the cinema screen in a blaze of bright colours, hot actors, outrageous costumes, sexy tableaux and tabloid-headline plots. Both Almódovar and Jarman inherited the Weimar association of QUILTBAG culture and lived experience with that of an urban underworld, or what Fred Moten and Stefano Harney call the 'undercommons', those excluded by poverty and/or predilection from normative bourgeois existence.

And that is where radical queer cinema has, to a great extent, been consigned by mainstream culture. *Now You See It*, as Richard Dyer titled his first full-length book on gay and lesbian cinema; the implication being ...and now you don't. The ambiguous figure holds. Mainstream film critics can lionise Almódovar while – by – ignoring, entirely, the radical queerness of his work, which satirises exactly the leonine auteurism in which the mainstream attempts to dress him up.

Almodóvar's work tells the secret he learned from the filmmakers who defined a post-war queer cinema rooted in leftist politics. Emerging from the social radicalism of Italian neo-realism was Pier Paolo Pasolini, an openly gay filmmaker in conservative post-war Italy, whose first novel and film faced censorship for obscenity and depictions of the criminal underworld. The *ragazzi* – street youth – of his early films become witnesses to the Crucifixion and the faces of fables in his mid-period; while in the revolutionary air of 1968 he cast Terence Stamp as a bisexual drifter in *Teorema*, a film that works out a theory of how to destroy the bourgeois family – and thus the conservative state – through queer *sexualwissenschaft*. His pansexual picaresque *Salò*, a cinematic take on the sexual politics of the Marquis de Sade and one of the most controversial films of all time, was made and released in 1975, the year of his murder, which has long been regarded as a state-ordered Mafia killing. His murderers called him a 'dirty communist' as they crushed his testicles with a metal bar, an *entartet*-style literalisation of his sexual(ity as) politics and their fear thereof.

Ten years later, the next great European queer filmmaker would die, after a career similarly pressed upon by political conservatives and media controversies. His overdose represents the social, as well as creative, pressures applied against his attempt to hold a mirror up to German corruption and complacency.

Born three weeks after the Nazis' unconditional surrender, in what would shortly become West Germany, Rainer Werner Fassbinder faced down his compatriots and pushed them to confront their complicity. Like Pasolini, he openly depicted queer communities and desires, the suppression of which persisted long after the end of the war. The often lurid, in-your-face energy of queer sexuality glows from Fassbinder's films, which share with Pasolini's an exploration of the undercommons, and which were cast from the director's all-embracing array of lovers and friends.

This disreputable repertory company drew on its own lived repertoire in order to queer European cultural heritage, in a rebuke to the conservatism of West Germany. Fassbinder's last film, in 1982, was an adaptation of Jean Genet's 1947 novel *Querelle de Brest*, a delirious vision of sailors in tight trousers. Its pastichey references to anti-Nazi romance *Casablanca* (Michael Curtiz, 1942), set amid atemporal, postcard-like settings and costumes, insist on a revisionist history of queerness that is at once specific – there were QUILTBAG people during (and since) WWII – and held secretly in the fold, like those of the bar's red curtains.

Fassbinder's mission was to unfold the curtains: in *Effi Briest* (1974), which adapts a Prussian novel about sexual blackmail written and set the year after Wilde's trial, the protagonist's parents famously dismiss their responsibility for her death. The filmmaker reads their casual and cowardly response to assert a continuum through imperial, Nazi and post-war Germanies.

It is this restatement of German complicity that fires Fassbinder's incredible productivity; his rage at continual erasure, one with no way out, drove him to make thirty-one films in just over two decades. His films hold a bitterly honest mirror up to post-war West Germany with their repeated, horrifically tragic endings under social pressure to conform. This pattern reaches its apotheosis of poignancy and frustration in *In The Year of Thirteen Moons* (1978). The film is Fassbinder's reaction to his lover Amin Meier's suicide (and one of the first films to feature a trans woman protagonist, as Juliet Jacques has noted). Like characters such as Effi and *Thirteen Moons*'s Elvira who collapses in a convent as she hears a nun (played by the filmmaker's mother) recount her brutal childhood, Fassbinder was sanctified only once he was safely (and tragically) dead, hagiographised as a one-man West German film industry.

What that canonisation has disguised is how his work created something like the bar in *Querelle*: a milieu in which QUILTBAG filmmakers and artists could flourish. He nurtured the early career of the first West German feminist filmmaker, Ula Stöckl, and it was his work that opened the doors for the German new queer wave, including East German lesbian filmmakers Monika Treut and Ulrike Ottinger, whose early works featuring BDSM and the lesbian undercommons ran headlong into 1980s Anglophone anti-sex feminism.

Rosa von Praunheim, who made the documentary *Fassbinder Was the Only One For Me: The Willing Victims of Rainer Werner F* (2000) about the late filmmaker's collaborators, became the bridge between New German Cinema and the American gay rights movement. His aptly titled 1971 documentary *It Is Not the Homosexual Who Is Perverse, But the Society in Which He Lives* led to the founding of the first gay rights organisations in German-speaking countries since Hirschfeld's exile forty years earlier. The film was influential in the nascent gay liberation movement in the US, where he subsequently went on to make radical films in the company of emerging filmmakers such as Barbara Hammer, whose explicit 1974 short *Dyketactics* irrevocably queered the visual language of cinema. Von Praunheim took the name 'Rosa' for the pink of the pink triangle, and his films were among the first texts to make the connection between genocidal Nazi policies and the repression by post-war liberal democracies of QUILTBAG identities and cultures.

HIGH PERFORMANCE

Why is Reverend Donald Wildmon Trying to Censor This Man?

It is a video you are not allowed to see. No one is allowed to see it.

In 2010, the National Portrait Gallery of the Smithsonian Institute in Washington DC mounted *Hide/Seek: Difference and Desire in American Portraiture*, billing itself as 'the first major museum exhibition to focus on sexual difference in the making of modern American portraiture.' The exhibition initially included a four-minute edit of a thirteen-minute 1987 video work by David Wojnarowicz.

A Fire in My Belly is an unfinished, silent experimental film shot on Super 8mm, looking at how the AIDS epidemic was ravaging Mexico. The four-minute edit originally appeared in von Praunheim's 1990 documentary *Silence=Death*, with Wojnarowicz and von Praunheim in conversation over three minutes of the footage. As ants crawl over a crucifix on screen, we hear Diamanda Galás' *Plague Mass*, composed and performed for people with AIDS.

'All my work', Galás recently said, is 'really from the point of view of the person who's been buried alive.' Burned alive, buried alive: the impossible non-choice of staying in the fire, screaming under the soil, underseen and underheard, or of entering the erasure of the white cube.

The Smithsonian exhibition appeared to argue that representation is politics; that visible difference, as tolerated by the institution, guarantees social transformation. However, a month after it opened, on World AIDS Day 2010, the gallery – one of the most influential and established national institutions in the US – succumbed to pressure from the Catholic League, who had mobilised Republican members of the House of Representatives, and removed the video from the exhibition. Nearly twenty years after his death from AIDS-related illness, Wojnarowicz was being silenced by the same conservative alliance that attempted to censor his work during his lifetime.

Wojnarowicz was one of several QUILTBAG artists whose response to the AIDS epidemic was to push at the limits of artistic representation in order to push through the social taboos and political oppressions that had, through wilful inaction, turned a virus into a global crisis. Wojnarowicz famously marched in 1988 wearing a denim jacket screenprinted with the message, 'IF I DIE OF AIDS – FORGET BURIAL – JUST DROP MY BODY ON THE STEPS OF THE F.D.A.' Beneath the white letters was the pink triangle that had become the pre-eminent symbol of the genocidal intent of the Republican administration's mishandling of AIDS under Reagan and Bush Sr.

Inspired by Wojnarowicz's imagining of a similar form of protest in his memoir *Close to the Knives*, in October 1992 members of ACT UP (AIDS Coalition to Unleash Power) spread the ashes of their late and mourned loved ones, including those of Wojnarowicz, on the lawn of the White House. It had taken nearly 50,000 deaths before Ronald Reagan even mentioned AIDS in public, in 1987. His government then perpetuated the eugenicist myth that only people dehumanised as the 'four Hs' – Haitians, homosexuals, heroin users and haemophiliacs – were at risk of AIDS, a racist, imperialist, homophobic, classist, ableist and essentialist (non-) grouping of those designated *entartet*. AIDS was framed as a degenerate disease only affecting those already labelled degenerate. It was a shameless strategy, a baseless and blood-stained taxonomy that the Nazis would have admired.

Facing a hostile government and medical-industrial complex, along with an equally hostile mass media, QUILTBAG activists revived and renewed the methods of earlier militant grassroots social justice movements. Like the Institut für Sexualwissenschaft, they took the scientific research that the straight community would not touch into their own hands, through the TAC, the Treatment Action Committee of ACT UP NY.

Central to ACT UP's actions, however, was public art, which ranged widely across forms to meet people where they needed to find it: in the street, where situationist and experimental performances disrupted Times Square matinée lines and church services; on free cable channels, where community video projects gave public health advice directly to the most isolated and marginalised communities; in short films, poems, essays, novels and plays that mostly circulated within queer and alternative communities long before AIDS was mentioned in the mainstream.

Like *Blue*, *A Fire In My Belly* has been sufficiently sanitised by the artist's death that it is now admitted to national institutions like the Smithsonian and the Whitney Museum, whose 2018 Wojnarowicz retrospective met with protests from the still-active ACT UP NY. 'AIDS is not history', read the flyer they distributed at the museum. 'Do not memorialize or romanticize the circumstances and activism of artists from oppressed groups.' Do not insist on trauma clowning; on softness as the only radicalism allowed. 2018 also saw the Smithsonian selling 'Silence=Death' T-shirts as part of its exhibition *Brand New: Art and Commodity in the 1980s*. This is a perfect example of what Walter Benjamin calls, in the coda to his 1935 essay 'The Work of Art in the Age of Mechanical Reproduction', the 'aestheticisation of politics', which he describes as one of the insidious operations of fascism.

Keith Haring's rage-fuelled use of the pink triangle in his ACT UP cartoons had been its own kind of accessible activism, reclaiming QUILTBAG history for the street in legible, impactful primary colours. His reclamation was, in Benjamin's counter-formation, a 'politicisation of aesthetics' that refused nostalgia or sentimentality. It offered a rejoinder to the reification of the Holocaust industry through solidarity, by linking struggles intergenerationally and across national borders, refusing exceptionalism.

Jarman's writing too – albeit in (red, hot and) blue rather than pink – performs what Haring's New York contemporary, queer theorist Douglas Crimp called 'militant melancholia' with reference to work such as Wojnarowicz's. Crimp argues that AIDS activists embraced the impossibility of mourning, which would denote a completed process, instead untapping the radical potential of melancholia as a form of ongoing, never-finished activism against multiple forms of repression, in both its political and psychoanalytic senses.

Folded time, in which the past is never fixed and can never be repressed, is a militantly melancholic practice, one that struggles against the kind of amnesiac repetitions caused by totalising narratives. *A Fire in My Belly* continues to push back against both censorship and canonisation through its militant melancholia, its unfinishedness that refuses to stay still and enfolds us into its own, always-urgent time.

Assimilation assimilates by erasing history. It smooths sense across the cut, refusing the startling charge of montage in favour of homogenisation. It insists on the authoritarian inscription of a single story – whether conservative or 'progressive' – told only in linear time.

Queer time enfolds personal and cultural histories in their full complexity, in their inclusion and their complicity in exclusion. By insisting we look hard at these stories frame by frame, it teaches us how to read across the gaps. By staying in the gaps for an electrifying moment.

Queer Lisboa 2019 opened with the Brazilian film *Indianara*, co-directed by Aude Chevalier-Beaumel and Marcelo Barbosa. The directors almost didn't make it for opening night, as a week earlier their funding disappeared when Jair Bolsonaro's fascist government revoked the national film ministry's grants for overseas travel, a move clearly and specifically targeted at queer filmmakers and festivals. A ripped-from-the-headlines documentary, *Indianara* runs to catch up with Indianara Siquiera, an activist, community-builder, politician, sex worker and friend of Marielle Franco, as she defends the squatted Casa Nem, which she occupied as a home for the trans, Black and Indigenous street-living Brazilian women who are her sisters to face down an authoritarian regime that openly wields the illogic of *entartet*. It was the first time a documentary had opened Queer Lisboa, and I was among the one thousand spectators who filled the main salon to bursting.

Screening the film, even with the directors defiantly present, was not enough to resist the history of cinema's complicity in perpetuating fascism and colonialism, to subvert or critique documentary's emergence from 'fascinating cannibalism', or film festival culture's participation in circuits of nationalist and commercial soft power that blunt political resistance. A beacon of radical potential in a recently fascist country, hosted in a cinema that houses the former censor's screening room, Queer Lisboa knew it had to activate the anarchive.

Thus the festival didn't open with the film, but with an unannounced performance by one of the activists who appears in it. Subject to officialdom and state funding, festivals and event screenings usually start with important bodies performing from the stage: Queer Lisboa made a radical departure. Biancka Fernandes, a performer and AIDS activist, descended through the auditorium from the back rows of the balcony, singing, preaching. Walking, in ball culture's sense. Her walk summoned me into what I call *activist* viewing, the kind of viewing insisted on by Eisenstein's theory of montage. Difference disrupts passive reception and calls us to attention; the plurality of meanings created by juxtapositions call us to action. *Indianara*'s breathless cinematic energy was a reminder that *cinéma vérité* was once an important formal and activist innovation, before it was normalised and co-opted by reality television. Fernandes's *sexualwissenschaft* read the film, and enabled us to read it for its urgent liveness.

Walking over and between us, Fernandes called out a prayer for us to protect her and her sisters – Indianara, her queer and trans family – from the Bolsonaro government that is determined to accelerate Brazil's half-millennium of colonial eradication. Her prayer also summoned and celebrated her own beauty and power, her living embodiment of continuity, her repertoire;

the world as it should be.

Dominance of the visual field is not just a question of representation, inclusive or otherwise. It is a structural and systemic practice, one that pervades technological as well as social and aesthetic change. As Pepper LaBeija, mother of the House of LaBeija, puts it in *Paris is Burning*:

> And when it come to the minorities, especially Black, we as a people, for the past 400 years, is the greatest example of behaviour modification in the history of civilization. We have had everything taken away from us and yet we have all learned how to survive. That is why, in the ballroom circuit, it is so obvious that if you have captured the great white way of living, or looking... or dressing or speaking – you is a marvel.

Overturning not only assumptions but also reality claims, ballroom culture and other QUILTBAG practices from the margins and the streets refuse 'the great white way', and so risk failure and re-erasure. They form not an archive, but an anarchive – a living and therefore unassimilable web of interconnections that can only be seen in fragments as they scintillate.

Artists like Bentley, Hammer, Jarman, Muholi, Fernandes and LaBeija are working and performing in a long tradition of queer resistance that knows, as Audre Lorde wrote, that the master's tools will never dismantle the master's house. The tools need to be dismantled first. This work is done, as Jarman puts it, at your own risk – what is at stake is your connection to precarious others, from whom dominant culture attempts to separate you.

The work is done by looking at – knowing that we are handling – nitrate: history and culture that are not inert but combustible. The official archives always contain explosive secrets. It is our prerogative as queer, trans, disabled, feminist, Black, Indigenous, decolonial anarchivists to access this nitrate, and to handle it with care for ourselves and our ancestors.

Not archive fever but the ache of archive love; archive desire; archive joy. Not keeping secrets but unfolding them.

'The only secret people keep is immortality.' An anarchive is a vision of immortality that offers an alternative to the monumental memorialising of state archives and official histories, through radical practices of folded time and embodied memory. It both prizes its attention to ephemera and shows off its militant melancholia for fragmentation and erasure.

Or, as Dorian Corey says in *Paris is Burning*:

> Everybody wants to make an impression, some mark upon the world. Then you think, you've made a mark on the world if you just get through it, and a few people remember your name. Then you've left a mark. You don't have to bend the whole world.

QUILTBAG communities and cultures have left their mark. Remember their names.

If we cannot learn our history in all its complexity, we cannot speak it. If we leave it unspoken, it risks erasure. Silence equals death, in ACT UP's famous formulation: for individuals, for communities, for worlds and lifeways. The history we carry is our history, each of us an anarchive, perhaps of untaken photographs and destroyed films, of work we will never have the opportunity to see or make, but also of the yearning to make that impossible work possible.

This is the secret we keep, people like us whom power tries to deny: that immortality lives in our continuous resistance.

Is in us; is us.

Ima Read

Introducing the bibliographic essay that closes his book *Why Indigenous Literatures Matter* (2018), Cherokee scholar Daniel Heath Justice writes that he 'wanted the bibliography not to be merely a list of sources, but a conversation about the embraided influence of words, ideas, and voices on the topic at hand' (242).

And equally, in the legendary words of Zebra Katz, the stage name of self-described 'Black, queer and "other"' artist and musician Ojay Morgan,

> I'm gonna take that bitch to college
> I'm gonna give that bitch some knowledge

This book is dedicated to everyone who gave me knowledge. 'Ima Read', Katz's 2013 underground hit, is a homage to the drag ball scene documented in *Paris is Burning*, and a reclamation of it for its Black, Latinx, queer and trans constituents. It's an instruction to look beyond the archive to the anarchive; to remember the genealogy of texts and sources out of which we're quilted, as individuals indivisibly in community; and how, in order to bring our selves, we need to bring them, as Justice says, into the conversation.

A Nazi Word for a Nazi Thing is quotation-lite, partially in order to centre visual artists and visual texts as ways of thinking through themselves and other things; and partially in order to take responsibility for my own thoughts. This is not a personal essay: and yet it is. My existence and experience are deeply implicated in the history of *entartet* and my survival depends on the solidarity I try to present and engage in; rather than account for or argue that through autobiography, I have instead focused on centring and connecting, in my own words, the anarchive of texts and practitioners that make me up. That is not to say that I own the words; it is also to recognise the anarchic aspects of thinking with a body of work that feels disparate because its potential for interconnection in solidarity has been repeatedly fractured by attempted erasures. Thus, each text I read arrived with the shock of montage, the juxtaposition demanding that I read into the gaps between them. Each reading here is an explosion.

Each picture in the text is uncaptioned to create a picture riddle, an opportunity for the reader to see it and interpret it for themselves, to open the possibility of connotation rather than denotation. As Carson's Geryon titles his untaken photograph, 'The Only Secret People Keep', he is quoting Emily Dickinson, who closes the couplet: '... Is immortality.' Attribution is also important. These are their sources:

- Image 1, p. 17: Book burning in Opernplatz, 10 May 1933, newsreel still, British Pathé
- Image 2, p. 25: Two frames from *Different From the Others* (Richard Oswald, 1919), showing Paul (Conrad Veidt) and the

Doctor (Magnus Hirschfeld) in consultation

- Image 3, p. 40: A page from the *Entartete 'Kunst'* exhibition catalogue (1937)
- Image 4, p. 43: 'My Wife or My Mother-in-Law' (William Ely Hill, 1915)
- Image 5, p. 61: Intertitle, frame from *Nitrate Kisses* (Barbara Hammer, 1992). Courtesy of the Barbara Hammer Estate and Electronic Arts Intermix (EAI), New York
- Image 6, p. 71: Gladys Bentley publicity postcard, signed by the artist
- Image 7, p. 74: Installation view, *Faces and Phases*, Stevenson Gallery, Johannesburg, 2016 (Zanele Muholi)
- Image 8, p. 94: Manuela defends her love to Fraulein von Bernburg, *Mädchen in Uniform* (Leontine Sagan, 1931). Courtesy of Kino Lorber
- Image 9, p. 104: Sergei Eisenstein seated on the Russian Imperial Throne (attrib. Alexander Sigaev, 1927)

- Image 10, p. 110: Derek Jarman, on the day he was 'canonised' at Dungeness, 22 September, 1991. Courtesy of Ed Sykes
- Image 11, p. 129: Cover of *High Performance: A Quarterly Magazine for the New Arts* 51 (Fall 1990), featuring a photograph of David Wojnarowicz by Andreas Sterzing, from the 'A Fire In My Belly' segment of the film *Silence=Death* by Rosa von Praunheim and Phil Zwickler (1990)
- Image 12, p. 140: Cast of *Paris is Burning* (Jennie Livingston, 1991): Back row: Angie Xtravaganza, Kim Pendavis, Pepper Labeija, Junior Labeija. Middle row: David Xtravaganza, Octavia St. Laurent, Dorian Corey, Willi Ninja. Front: Freddie Pendavis. Courtesy of Janus Films

I once read an essay about picture captions where, for 'denotation', there was the repeated typo *detonation*. I feel that. Sometimes spell-check automatism gives us what we didn't know we needed. A text or an image that makes meaning explodes it; explodes me. It reads where I'm lacking and calls me to do better. All the texts below detonate both conventional disciplines and the uncategorical categories in which I've brought them together. Read them because you cannot read without them.

Category Is... Queer/Jewish/Other

The total American dominance of this list speaks to the dominance of both QUILTBAG and Ashkenazi Jewish international post-war culture by American thought and practice. These books think differently, though; in solidarity and against capitalist and imperial versions of *entartet*.

- Judith Butler, *Parting Ways: Jewishness and the Critique of Zionism*
- Noach Dzmurah, ed. *Balancing on the Mechitza: Transgender in Jewish Community*
- Leslie Feinberg, *Stone Butch Blues*
- Sander Gilman, *The Jew's Body*
- Melanie Kaye/Kantrowitz, *The Colors of*

Jews: Racial Politics and Radical Diasporism

- Ann Pellegrini, Daniel Boyarin, and Daniel Itzkovitz, eds. *Queer Theory and the Jewish Question*
- Rebecca Walker, *Black, White and Jewish: Autobiography of a Shifting Self*

Category Is... Reading Berlin

From Hirschfeld to Haritaworn, the literature on Berlin as queer margin/centre is vast and still (as in Hájková's work) emerging from the anarchives, via which Edugyan and Olusoga differently shed light on Black Berlins.

- Richard Beachy, *Gay Berlin*
- Esi Edugyan, *Half Blood Blues*
- Anja Hájková, *Boundaries of the Narratable: Transgressive Sexuality and the Holocaust* (forthcoming) and her research on lesbian and bisexual women in the Nazi era at https://sexualityandholocaust.com/blog/bibliography/
- Jin Haritaworn, *Queer Lovers and Hate-*

ful Others: Regenerating Violent Times and Places
- Magnus Hirschfeld, *Berlin's Third Sex*
- David Olusoga, *The World's War: Forgotten Soldiers of Empire*

Category Is... Anarchives

The archive is at the heart of the work of decolonisation, for what it holds and what it omits, what it obscures and what it (often unwillingly) permits. Finding, formulating and forwarding anarchives is what I've learned from these scholars.

- Ariella Azoulay, *Potential History: Unlearning Imperialism*
- Pearl Bowser, *Oscar Micheaux and His Circle: African-American Filmmaking and Race Cinema of the Silent Era*
- Ann Cvetkovich, *An Archive of Feelings: Trauma, Sexuality and Lesbian Public Cultures*
- Anne McClintock, *Imperial Leather: Race,*

Gender and Sexuality in the Colonial Conquest

- Saidiya Hartman, *Wayward Lives, Beautiful Experiments: Intimate Histories of Riotous Black Girls, Troublesome Women and Queer Radicals*
- Achille Mbembe, 'Decolonizing Knowledge and the Question of the Archive'
- Fatimah Tobing Rony, *The Third Eye: Race, Cinema, and Ethnographic Spectacle*
- Sarah Schulman, ACT UP Oral History Project at http://www.actuporalhistory.org
- Diana Taylor, *The Archive and the Repertoire: Performing Cultural Memory in the Americas*

Category Is... Stay Radical

Insights and incitements are everywhere. These are a few of the many to which I return, for their engagement with the first person (plural) speculative in all its (im)possibilities. Being numerous is, as Lennard writes, necessary, and each of these texts will lead you to a community of more.

- Chimamanda Ngozi Adichie, 'The Danger of a Single Story', TEDGlobal, July 2009, https://www.ted.com/talks/chimamanda_ngozi_adichie_the_danger_of_a_single_story
- Walter Benjamin, 'The Work of Art in the Age of Mechanical Reproduction', trans. Harry Zohn
- Lizzie Borden, *Born in Flames*
- Helen Charman, 'Where Do I Put Myself, If Public Life's Destroyed? On Reading Denise Riley'
- Masha Gessen, *The Future is History: How Totalitarianism Reclaimed Russia*
- Donna Haraway, 'A Cyborg Manifesto: Science, Technology and Socialist-Feminism in the Late Twentieth Century'
- Ursula K. Le Guin, *The Carrier Bag Theory of Fiction*
- Natasha Lennard, *Being Numerous: Essays*

on Non-Fascist Life
- Fred Moten and Stefan Harney, *The Undercommons: Fugitive Planning and Black Study*
- Vivek Shraya, 'How Did the Suffering of Marginalized Artists Become So Marketable?'
- Leanne Betasamosake Simpson, *As We Have Always Done: Indigenous Freedom through Radical Resistance*

Category Is... Decolonial Genders and Sexualities

This list is a line of flight, a community of connection, a promise of futures rich with histories. These, of all the books listed, are those that have most educated (and excited) me to see differently, and to see beyond and through what might be called 'my' history differently.

- Qwo-Li Driskill, Daniel Heath Justice, Deborah Miranda, and Lisa Tatonetti, eds. *Sovereign Erotics: A Collection of*

Two-Spirit Literature

- Sokari Ekine, ed. *Queer African Reader*
- Rita Indiana, *Tentacle*, translated by Achy Obejas
- Audre Lorde, *Your Silence Will Not Protect You*
- José Esteban Muñoz, *Disidentifications: Queers of Color and the Performance of Politics*
- Lola Olufemi, *Feminism, Interrupted: Disrupting Power*
- Nisha Ramayya, *States of the Body Produced by Love*
- Joan Roughgarden, *Evolution's Rainbow: Diversity, Gender, and Sexuality in Nature and People*
- Banu Subramaniam, *Ghost Stories for Darwin: The Science of Variation and the Politics of Diversity*
- Omise'eke Natasha Tinsley, *Ezili's Mirrors: Imagining Black Queer Genders*

Category Is... Queer Screens

My Mastermind special subject, so I've tried to keep it brief. And failed. Writing about queer audiovisual culture is both dynamic and significant because the works considered are often hard to see. When it comes to queer film, ironically, you have to read to see it.

- Anne Carson, *Autobiography of Red*
- Sarah Crewe and Pascal O'Loughlin, *RWF/RAF*
- Richard Dyer, *Now You See It: Studies on Gay and Lesbian Film*
- Martha Gever, John Greyson, and Pratibha Parmar, eds. *Queer Looks: Perspectives on Lesbian and Gay Film and Video*
- Barbara Hammer, *Hammer! Making Movies Out of Sex and Life*
- Pamela Hutchinson, *Pandora's Box* (BFI Film Classics)
- Derek Jarman, *Up in the Air: Collected Film Scripts*
- Juliet Jacques, *Trans: A Memoir*

- Kara Keeling, *The Witch's Flight: The Cinematic, the Black Femme and the Image of Common Sense*
- B Ruby Rich, *Chick Flicks: Theories and Memories of the Feminist Film Movement*
- Susan Stryker, 'Transsexuality: The Postmodern Body and/as Technology'
- Trinh T. Minh-Ha, *When the Moon Waxes Red: Representation, Gender and Cultural Politics*

Peninsula Press would like to thank Larry Coppersmith and Dominic Franklin for their continued support.